C000178341

ISBN 978-1-331-88387-6
PIBN 10249526

Elementary Classics.

Virgil

(P. VERGILI MARONIS AENEIDOS LIB. IV.

Edited for the use of Schools,

BY THE

REV. H. M. STEPHENSON, M.A.

VICAR OF BOURN, CAMBS.,
LATE HEADMASTER OF ST PETER'S SCHOOL, YORK,
FORMERLY FELLOW OF CHRIST'S COLLEGE, CAMBRIDGE.

WITH INTRODUCTION, NOTES AND VOCABULARY.

London:
MACMILLAN AND CO.
AND NEW YORK.
1888

Cambridge
PRINTED BY C. J. CLAY, M.A. & SONS
AT THE UNIVERSITY PRESS.

PREFACE.

The plan of this little book is the same as that of the Ninth Aeneid, published a short time ago. Here again I wish to refer students for information about Vergil's Life and poems in general, and the Fourth Aeneid in particular, to Prof. Nettleship's 'Vergil' in the 'Classical Writers' series.

The authority occasionally referred to by the abbreviation Kv., is Prof. Kvičala of the University of Prague.

The Text is mainly that of Mr Sidgwick's edition and is used by kind permission of the Syndics of the Cambridge University Press.

H. M. S.

Bourn, *April* 1888.

INTRODUCTION.

Diction of Vergil.

THE feature which strikes us most in the style or *form* of Vergil's verse as compared for example with that of Lucretius or Catullus, is its fulness and richness, its weight and solidity, or, to borrow a metaphor from wine-making, the full-bodied quality of it. The others flow on in a limpid stream, tripping and pleasant and easy and natural, but their stream is not very deep, there is not much weight of water in it. Vergil advances like the Rutulians in his own verses:

> Ceu septem surgens sedatis amnibus altus
> Per tacitum Ganges, aut pingui flumine Nilus
> Cum refluit campis et iam se condidit alveo.
>
> IX. 30.

It is this fulness and volume, this sustained stateliness of the Vergilian verse (not in the least incompatible, by the way, with extreme simplicity where simplicity is required) that makes it what it is. And this is the result of the combination of three elements, rhythm, arrangement and diction. It is intended in this Introduction (the object of which is simply to aid beginners in Hexameter versification) to deal only with the last-named element, and in regard to that, only with some of the mechanical appliances (so to say) which Vergil used to produce it.

For in order to secure the varied fulness of diction at which he aimed, it was necessary for Vergil to embody in it all that was available for poetic purposes in the Roman language, or as much of it as possible. And in order to effect this, it was necessary to adopt means to bring more of the language within the metrical possibilities of hexameter verse, than his predecessors had done.

It must however be carefully borne in mind, that in choosing these means Vergil was guided by a true and great poetic genius. The linguistic instruments he adopted therefore are not to be considered as adopted merely *metri gratia*, as devices to facilitate versification. Metrically useful they are, but no less poetically happy. In fact, while from one point of view they may be regarded as facilitating versification, from another they are distinct advances in poetic expression, means of attaining to a higher perfection of poetic language and improving poetic form, no less than appliances to bring more words within the range of hexameter verse. It is in the latter aspect however that they are considered in this Introduction.

The first of these appliances to be noticed is

I. The use of the enclitic conjunction *que*.

(The frequency of Vergil's use of this word may be judged by the fact that whereas in the whole of the Peleus and Thetis of Catullus it occurs only 17 times, and in two passages of 400 lines each taken at random from Lucretius, 52 and 42 times respectively, in the first 400 lines of this book it occurs 94 times.)

It is used, besides its *ordinary* copulative sense:

(*a*) To combine a principal and accessory statement instead of the more ordinary use of a participial or other subordinate clause (hendiadys of sentence), e.g. 76, 101, 119 &c. In the form hysteron proteron, 155.

(*b*) In hendiadys proper; i.e., the use of two *words* coordinated instead of an expression in which one qualifies the other grammatically, e.g. 26, 99, &c.

(c) In apposition; (1) epexegetic 103, 354, esp. in the form of double *que*, or *que* followed by *et*: 88, 94. (2) by way of particularising an individual thing of a group, or the part of a whole, 143, 507, 544.

(*d*) In anaphora, 3, 169, 437.

II. The Ablative case. Vergil's undefined and suggestive use of this case is a most remarkable feature in his style and furnishes a frequent metrical solvent.

It is used

(*a*) As the equivalent of an adjective or participle or ablative absolute: 72 (*fuga* = *fugiens*), 131, 212 (*pretio* = *pretio dato*). In two cases in this book the abl. = *dum* and a verb; 240 *sublimem alis* = *dum volat sublimis*: 649, *lacrimis* &c. = *dum lacrimis et menti indulgeat*.

This usage is specially noticeable where an abl. combined with a participle or neuter verb is practically equivalent to two or more adjectives qualifying the same substantive; 42 *deserta siti regio*. Here *siti* may be grammatically explained as abl. of cause, or circumstance, or both, and something more besides; practically it = *arida*. So 176 *parva metu* = *parva et metuens*. In 262, *Tyrio* &c., what is really signified is that Aeneas' *laena* was a blaze of bright, costly purple.

Under this head may be noticed a form of expression by which an action instead of being expressed in regard to the recipient of it by a passive verb and abl. of instrument is expressed by an independent circumstantial abl. with its own predicate, e.g. 69, *coniectâ sagittâ* = *ictă sagittâ*. Cf. 120, 198, 444, 701.

(*b*) Where ordinary usage would require another case: 110, 505.

III. The omission of the auxiliary verb *sum* in subordinate clauses: 80, 151. In the case of relative sentences the sentence = an adj. in oblique case.

Under this head may be noticed the use of *quam* and an adj. with or without the verb *sum* equivalent to an emphatic or intensified sense of the adj. 193. Cf. VIII. 86, Thybris ea fluvium, quam longa est, nocte tumentem Leniit.

IV. The use of adverbs qualifying substantives: 526.

V. Graecism:

(*a*) In construction:

(1) accus. after pf. pass. part.: 137, 493, 509, &c.

(2) accus. of part affected after adjs.: 558.

(3) Greek use of other cases: 178.

(4) infin. after adjs.: 564.

(5) infin. of purpose, where strict Latin construction would require *ut* with subjunctive: 575.

(6) condensed interrogative, or interrogative contained in a subordinate clause: 11, 14, 371.

(*b*) Greek forms: *Mnesthea* (288) &c.

VI. Archaism:

(*a*) form: 606.

(*b*) quantity: 64, 222.

VII. Use of plural for singular: 28, 43, 47, 59, 66, 82, 118, 135, 225, &c.

VIII. Synecdoche, that is, the expression of a whole by a characteristic part; 132.

IX. Personification. This figure in its general sense is common of course to all poetry, or rather forms the basis of all poetic expression. But one form of it, if not originated by Vergil, was so extended and so largely and freely used by him, that it seems natural to reckon it as a feature of his style. This is the form by which an attribute or circumstance or part of a person is identified with the person and qualified by an epithet strictly speaking only applicable to the person; as when Dido's eyes (364) and wound (67) are called 'silent,' her hands 'pious' (517), the fire that consumes her, 'blind' &c.

X. Vivid use of Indicative in conditional sentences, 19.

The young versifier will readily understand that these usages amongst others considerably facilitate the formation of the hexameter verse. For example, such a phrase as 'the world of waters deep and dark' is readily adapted to the requirements of hexameter verse by combining two substantives with *que*; *molem noctemque profundam*, (*tenebrasque profundas*). 'A broken chancel with a broken cross,' quite impracticable in its English form, is easily shaped if expressed by ablatives qualifying a participle agreeing with the 'chapel' in the previous line; 'quassatà desertam arâ fractisque columnis.' 'All day long' is not so manageable translated *toto die* as *quam longa dies* or *die quam longa* (*est*). But he will not if he is wise trust to such instruments alone in producing hexameters. They will be useful implements but only when guided by careful and loving study of Vergil himself.

A few pieces of translation are added from this book into English blank verse, and from English into hexameters, not by any means as models of translation, but simply by way of illustrating some of the remarks made above.

68—73.

Unhappy queen! A fire is in her heart,
Which drives her wild to roam the city's length;
Like wounded doe, surprised in Cretan woods,
The victim of a distant shot well-sped,
Shot by a shepherd, sporting with his bow;
He knows not that his wingèd bolt has lodg'd;
But she through glade and grove flies wildly on
Nor shakes the fatal arrow from her side.

174—177.

Rumour the swiftest curse that treads this earth;
Movement is life to her: each step adds strength:
Shrinking and small at first, anon she tow'rs,
'Her feet on earth, her forehead in the clouds.'

151—155, 160, 1.

When, now they reach the lairs amid the hills,
See! the wild goats from craggy brow dislodged

Shoot down the hillsides; there on the other side
Leaving the hills in huddled dusty pack
The startled deer fly o'er the spreading plain.
Thunder meanwhile makes tumult in the sky,
And quick the storm-cloud bursts in hail and rain.

229.

Land of the battle-cry, with empire big.

504—508.

Meanwhile within the halls the pyre is raised,
A tow'ring pile of pine and oaken logs;
The queen with wreaths of funeral festoon
Dresses the chamber; high on the pile-top
Her soldier's relics, and forgotten sword,
And sculptur'd form she lays, facing her doom.

522—532.

Night: and the weary world slept lapped in peace;
Hushed were the forests and fierce seas, the hour
When silent stars are half way on their course,
And ev'ry field is still, still flocks and herds,
And gay-plumed birds—birds of the spreading mere
And birds of the thorny brakes—all laid to rest
Beneath the silent canopy of night.
But not the heart-broken queen—She cannot lull
Her racked nerves into slumber; nor the night
Has no gift for her fevered eyes and brain.
Her sorrows double, and surging wave on wave
The tempest of her passion sweeps her soul.

MILTON, *Paradise Lost*, III. 1—12.

Salve, caelestis proles Lux prima Parentis!
Seu recte comitem Clari per saecula claram
Te licet appellare Dei; namque ipse Deus Lux,
Nec nisi inaccessum lumen praecinctus ab aevo
Splendet, nempe tuum, aeterni Splendoris imago

Splendida. An aetherii fluctus vis laetius audis,
Fonte fluens cui dicendo? Nam caerula nondum
Sole tenente poli fulges, quae iussa tenebras
Iam concrescentis ponti molemque profundam,
Informis modo quae iacuit nec in omne patenti
Rapta Chao, ornasti ceu veste effusa nitenti.

TENNYSON, *Morte d'Arthur*, 1—26.

*Martis ea quam longa die clamore resultant
Qui maris hiberni despectant aequora colles,
Dum comites regis, iuvenum fortissimus ordo,
Fato quisque suo pereunt, ducente feroces
Arturo; ast illum letali volnere fessum
Baedivir, ex illa qui clade superfuit unus,
Avexit sublimem umeris; dein ocius aedem
Haud procul a campo petiit, quae lapsa ruina,
Dimidia desertam ara, fractisque columnis;
Qua medium terra in dorsum nigrescit ab undis;
Oceanus patet hinc, illinc extenta paludis
Planities plena lunae sub luce coruscat.
Tum sic adfatur comitem rex ore locutus:
"Heu! Collapsa iacet virtus; tot fortia bello
Pectora queis pariter nulli socia arma tulere,
Quorum exstat iam fama, dies haec perdidit una.
A! fortes animae, qui vos sopor occupat altus!
Nam nos, credo equidem, non iam redeuntibus annis,
Ut quondam, patriae nota inter tecta vagantes,
Sive horti placuere, virum fortissima facta
Quemque sui comitis laudes memorare juvabit.
Ipse sui auctorem populus me perdit; at ille
Fata canens olim reduci regna altera vates
Promisit; sed enim regni quaecumque futuri
Sors maneat, trahere in lucem, quae proxima, vitam
Vix potero solus; tali sum saucius ictu."

* *Al.* Marte illa rauco quam longa est luce resultant.

The same. Last eight lines.

Dixerat; at remoque ratis ventoque secundo
Litore delapsa est, qualis feralia fundens
Carmina sub mortem curvato pectore cygnus
Remigio liquidas plantarum innixus in undas
Candidus exsultat, motasque superbit in alas.
Stabat multa diu memori sub corde volutans
Baedivir. Interea ratis in minus usque recedens
Exoriente die vix iam conspecta nigrabat;
Lugentumque cadunt voces; silet undique marmor.

Then all was well.
Sound was the body, and the soul serene;
Like two sweet instruments, ne'er out of tune,
That play their several parts—Nor head, nor heart,
Offered to ache; nor was there cause they should;
For all was pure within; no fell remorse
Nor anxious castings-up of what should be,
Alarmed his peaceful bosom—Summer seas
Show not more smooth when kissed by southern winds
Just ready to expire—Scarce importuned
The generous soil with a luxurious hand
Offered the various produce of the year,
And everything most perfect in its kind.

O felix tunc ille, animum qui corpore sano
Securum exhibuit! cithara sic dividit apta
Carmina dulcisona cantor; vis viva cerebri
Tunc ultro viguit, tunc corda oblita dolendi.
Nec mirum caeca qui purus labe carebat;
Namque illi sceleris prisci non cura remordens
Non nimium prudens animus metuensque futuri
Pectora sollicito potuit turbare quieta.
Non aestiva magis requiescunt aequora ponti,
Ultima queis Zephyrus moriens premit oscula fessis.
At tellus generosa manu et laetata benigna
Diversas anni fruges, quaeque optima promit
Munera quodque genus, vix sollicitata profudit.

P. VERGILI MARONIS
AENEIDOS

LIBER QUARTUS.

Vv. 1—30. *The queen Dido, deeply smitten with love for Aeneas, after passing a sleepless night confides her trouble to her sister Anna, confessing her passion, but vowing that nothing shall induce her to be untrue to the memory of her first husband.*

AT regina gravi iamdudum saucia cura
volnus alit venis, et caeco carpitur igni.
multa viri virtus animo, multusque recursat
gentis honos; haerent infixi pectore voltus
verbaque, nec placidam membris dat cura quietem.
postera Phoebea lustrabat lampade terras,
umentemque Aurora polo dimoverat umbram,
cum sic unanimam adloquitur male sana sororem:
'Anna soror, quae me suspensam insomnia terrent?
'quis novus hic nostris successit sedibus hospes?
'quem sese ore ferens! quam forti pectore et armis!
'credo equidem, nec vana fides, genus esse deorum:
'degeneres animos timor arguit. heu, quibus ille
'iactatus fatis quae bella exhausta canebat!

'si mihi non animo fixum immotumque sederet
'ne cui me vinclo vellem sociare iugali,
'postquam primus amor deceptam morte fefellit;
'si non pertaesum thalami taedaeque fuisset,
'huic uni forsan potui succumbere culpae.
'Anna, fatebor enim, miseri post fata Sychaei
'coniugis et sparsos fraterna caede penates,
'solus hic inflexit sensus, animumque labantem
'inpulit: adgnosco veteris vestigia flammae.
'sed mihi vel tellus optem prius ima dehiscat,
'vel Pater omnipotens adigat me fulmine ad umbras,
'pallentes umbras Erebi noctemque profundam,
'ante, Pudor, quam te violo, aut tua iura resolvo.
'ille meos, primus qui me sibi iunxit, amores
'abstulit; ille habeat secum servetque sepulchro.'
sic effata sinum lacrimis implevit obortis.

Vv. 31—55. *Anna in reply deprecates the perpetual widowhood to which Dido would condemn herself: 'the dead man will not care for what she does: her duty to the living requires that she should seize such an opportunity of strengthening her kingdom, disregard the apparent inconsistency of having rejected other suitors, and marry the man whom interest and inclination alike recommend to her: all that is necessary is to obtain the consent of the gods.'*

Anna refert: 'o luce magis dilecta sorori,
'solane perpetua maerens carpere iuventa,
'nec dulces natos, Veneris nec praemia noris?
'id cinerem aut manes credis curare sepultos?
'esto, aegram nulli quondam flexere mariti,

'non Libyae, non ante Tyro; despectus Iarbas,
'ductoresque alii, quos Africa terra triumphis
'dives alit: placitone etiam pugnabis amori?
'nec venit in mentem, quorum consederis arvis?
'hinc Gaetulae urbes, genus insuperabile bello,
'et Numidae infreni cingunt, et inhospita Syrtis;
'hinc deserta siti regio, lateque furentes
'Barcaei. quid bella Tyro surgentia dicam
'germanique minas?
'dis equidem auspicibus reor et Iunone secunda
'hunc cursum Iliacas vento tenuisse carinas.
'quam tu urbem, soror, hanc cernes, quae surgere regna
'coniugio tali! Teucrum comitantibus armis,
'Punica se quantis attollet gloria rebus!
'tu modo posce deos veniam, sacrisque litatis
'indulge hospitio, causasque innecte morandi,
'dum pelago desaevit hiemps et aquosus Orion,
'quassataeque rates, dum non tractabile caelum.'
his dictis incensum animum inflammavit amore,
spemque dedit dubiae menti, solvitque pudorem.

Vv. 56—89. *Accordingly they sacrifice, and consult the gods by* extispicium. *Uselessly: for her mind is already made up: no offices of religion can cure her passion: she is blind to omens: she gives herself up wholly to her love: day and evening she spends with Aeneas: at night she mourns alone in the palace. All the works of the city are suspended.*

Principio delubra adeunt, pacemque per aras
exquirunt: mactant lectas de more bidentes

legiferae Cereri Phoeboque patrique Lyaeo,
Iunoni ante omnes, cui vincla iugalia curae.
ipsa, tenens dextra pateram, pulcherrima Dido
candentis vaccae media inter cornua fundit;
aut ante ora deum pingues spatiatur ad aras,
instauratque diem donis, pecudumque reclusis
pectoribus inhians spirantia consulit exta.
heu vatum ignarae mentes! quid vota furentem,
quid delubra iuvant? est molles flamma medullas
interea, et tacitum vivit sub pectore volnus.
uritur infelix Dido totaque vagatur
urbe furens, qualis coniecta cerva sagitta,
quam procul incautam nemora inter Cresia fixit
pastor agens telis, liquitque volatile ferrum
nescius: illa fuga silvas saltusque peragrat
Dictaeos; haeret lateri letalis arundo.
nunc media Aenean secum per moenia ducit,
Sidoniasque ostentat opes urbemque paratam;
incipit effari, mediaque in voce resistit:
nunc eadem labente die convivia quaerit,
Iliacosque iterum demens audire labores
exposcit, pendetque iterum narrantis ab ore.
post, ubi digressi, lumenque obscura vicissim
luna premit, suadentque cadentia sidera somnos,
sola domo maeret vacua, stratisque relictis
incubat: illum absens absentem auditque videtque
aut gremio Ascanium, genitoris imagine capta,
detinet, infandum si fallere possit amorem.
non coeptae adsurgunt turres; non arma iuventus

exercet, portusve aut propugnacula bello
tuta parant: pendent opera interrupta, minaeque
murorum ingentes, aequataque machina caelo.

Vv. 90—104. *Juno seeing her helpless state proposes to Venus to bring about a marriage, and establish a joint empire of Trojans and Carthaginians.*

Quam simul ac tali persensit peste teneri
cara Iovis coniunx, nec famam obstare furori,
talibus adgreditur Venerem Saturnia dictis:
'egregiam vero laudem et spolia ampla refertis
'tuque puerque tuus, magnum et memorabile nomen,
'una dolo divom si femina victa duorum est.
'nec me adeo fallit, veritam te moenia nostra
'suspectas habuisse domos Carthaginis altae.
'sed quis erit modus? aut quo nunc certamine tanto?
'quin potius pacem aeternam pactosque hymenaeos
'exercemus? habes, tota quod mente petisti:
'ardet amans Dido traxitque per ossa furorem.
'communem hunc ergo populum paribusque regamus
'auspiciis; liceat Phrygio servire marito,
'dotalisque tuae Tyrios permittere dextrae.'

Vv. 105—128. *Venus sees through the design to divert the Trojan empire to Carthage but consents, subject to Jupiter's approval. Juno will see to that: she instructs Venus how the marriage is to be brought about by means of the hunt and the thunderstorm.*

Olli—sensit enim simulata mente locutam,
quo regnum Italiae Libycas averteret oras—

sic contra est ingressa Venus: 'quis talia demens
'abnuat, aut tecum malit contendere bello,
'si modo, quod memoras, factum fortuna sequatur?
'sed fatis incerta feror, si Iuppiter unam
'esse velit Tyriis urbem Troiaque profectis,
'miscerive probet populos, aut foedera iungi.
'tu coniunx; tibi fas animum temptare precando.
'perge; sequar.' tum sic excepit regia Iuno:
'mecum erit iste labor. nunc qua ratione, quod instat,
'confieri possit, paucis, adverte, docebo.
'venatum Aeneas unaque miserrima Dido
'in nemus ire parant, ubi primos crastinus ortus
'extulerit Titan radiisque retexerit orbem.
'hic ego nigrantem commixta grandine nimbum,
'dum trepidant alae, saltusque indagine cingunt,
'desuper infundam, et tonitru caelum omne ciebo.
'diffugient comites, et nocte tegentur opaca:
'speluncam Dido dux et Troianus eandem
'devenient. adero, et, tua si mihi certa voluntas,
'conubio iungam stabili propriamque dicabo.
'hic Hymenaeus erit.' non adversata petenti
adnuit, atque dolis risit Cytherea repertis.

Vv. 129—159. *Dawn the next day: preparations for the hunt. All are waiting for the Queen who at last comes forth in rich apparel and is presently joined by Aeneas. Then the hunting begins, Ascanius specially distinguishing himself.*

Oceanum interea surgens Aurora relinquit.
it portis iubare exorto delecta iuventus:

retia rara, plagae, lato venabula ferro,
Massylique ruunt equites, et odora canum vis.
reginam thalamo cunctantem ad limina primi
Poenorum exspectant, ostroque insignis et auro
stat sonipes, ac frena ferox spumantia mandit.
tandem progreditur magna stipante caterva
Sidoniam picto chlamydem circumdata limbo:
cui pharetra ex auro, crines nodantur in aurum,
aurea purpuream subnectit fibula vestem.
nec non et Phrygii comites et laetus Iulus
incedunt. ipse ante alios pulcherrimus omnes
infert se socium Aeneas, atque agmina iungit.
qualis ubi hibernam Lyciam Xanthique fluenta
deserit, ac Delum maternam invisit Apollo,
instauratque choros, mixtique altaria circum
Cretesque Dryopesque fremunt pictique Agathyrsi:
ipse iugis Cynthi graditur, mollique fluentem
fronde premit crinem fingens, atque inplicat auro;
tela sonant umeris: haud illo segnior ibat
Aeneas; tantum egregio decus enitet ore.
postquam altos ventum in montes atque invia lustra,
ecce ferae, saxi deiectae vertice, caprae
decurrere iugis; alia de parte patentes
transmittunt cursu campos atque agmina cervi
pulverulenta fuga glomerant montesque relinquunt.
at puer Ascanius mediis in vallibus acri
gaudet equo, iamque hos cursu, iam praeterit illos,
spumantemque dari pecora inter inertia votis
optat aprum, aut fulvom descendere monte leonem.

Vv. 160—172. *Presently the storm comes on. Dido and Aeneas seek shelter in a cave, where their marriage is accomplished. Dido now claims to be his lawful wife.*

Interea magno misceri murmure caelum
incipit; insequitur commixta grandine nimbus.
et Tyrii comites passim et Troiana iuventus
Dardaniusque nepos Veneris diversa per agros
tecta metu petiere: ruunt de montibus amnes.
speluncam Dido dux et Troianus eandem
deveniunt. prima et Tellus et pronuba Iuno
dant signum: fulsere ignes, et conscius aether
conubiis, summoque ulularunt vertice Nymphae.
ille dies primus leti primusque malorum
causa fuit. neque enim specie famave movetur,
nec iam furtivum Dido meditatur amorem:
coniugium vocat; hoc praetexit nomine culpam.

Vv. 173—197. *The news is spread all over Libya b[illegible] monster Rumour, who is here described. She carries an exaggerated tale of the loves of Dido and Aeneas to Iarbas a rejected suitor of the Queen.*

Extemplo Libyae magnas it Fama per urbes,
Fama, malum qua non aliud velocius ullum:
mobilitate viget, viresque adquirit eundo;
parva metu primo; mox sese attollit in auras,
ingrediturque solo, et caput inter nubila condit.
illam Terra parens, ira inritata deorum,
extremam, ut perhibent, Coeo Enceladoque sororem
progenuit, pedibus celerem et pernicibus alis;

monstrum horrendum, ingens, cui quot sunt corpore plumae,
tot vigiles oculi subter, mirabile dictu,
tot linguae, totidem ora sonant, tot subrigit aures.
nocte volat caeli medio terraeque per umbram
stridens, nec dulci declinat lumina somno.
luce sedet custos aut summi culmine tecti,
turribus aut altis, et magnas territat urbes,
tam ficti pravique tenax quam nuntia veri.
haec tum multiplici populos sermone replebat
gaudens et pariter facta atque infecta canebat:
venisse Aenean, Troiano a sanguine cretum,
cui se pulchra viro dignetur iungere Dido;
nunc hiemem inter se luxu, quam longa, fovere,
regnorum inmemores turpique cupidine captos.
haec passim dea foeda virum diffundit in ora.
protinus ad regem cursus detorquet Iarban,
incenditque animum dictis, atque aggerat iras.

Vv. 198—218. *This king, son of Jupiter Ammon, indignant at the news, makes his prayer to his father, demanding vengeance on* Dido, '*if Jupiter's power is not a fiction and all his temples and altars built in vain.*'

Hic Hammone satus, rapta Garamantide nympha,
templa Iovi centum latis immania regnis,
centum aras posuit, vigilemque sacraverat ignem,
excubias divom aeternas, pecudumque cruore
pingue solum, et variis florentia limina sertis.
isque amens animi, et rumore accensus amaro,

dicitur ante aras, media inter numina divom,
multa Iovem manibus supplex orasse supinis:
'Iuppiter omnipotens, cui nunc Maurusia pictis
'gens epulata toris Lenaeum libat honorem,
'aspicis haec? an te, genitor, cum fulmina torques,
'nequiquam horremus, caecique in nubibus ignes
'terrificant animos, et inania murmura miscent?
'femina, quae nostris errans in finibus urbem
'exiguam pretio posuit, cui litus arandum,
'cuique loci leges dedimus, conubia nostra
'repulit, ac dominum Aenean in regna recepit.
'et nunc ille Paris, cum semiviro comitatu,
'Maeonia mentum mitra crinemque madentem
'subnexus, rapto potitur: nos munera templis
'quippe tuis ferimus, famamque fovemus inanem.'

Vv. 219—237. *Jupiter at once charges Mercury to go and seek Aeneas, rebuke him for his folly, remind him of his destiny and bid him sail away at once.*

Talibus orantem dictis arasque tenentem
audiit omnipotens, oculosque ad moenia torsit
regia, et oblitos famae melioris amantes.
tum sic Mercurium adloquitur, ac talia mandat:
'vade age, nate, voca Zephyros, et labere pinnis,
'Dardaniumque ducem, Tyria Carthagine qui nunc
'exspectat, fatisque datas non respicit urbes,
'adloquere, et celeres defer mea dicta per auras.
'non illum nobis genetrix pulcherrima talem
'promisit, Graiumque ideo bis vindicat armis;

'sed fore, qui gravidam imperiis belloque frementem
'Italiam regeret, genus alto a sanguine Teucri
'proderet, ac totum sub leges mitteret orbem.
'si nulla accendit tantarum gloria rerum,
'nec super ipse sua molitur laude laborem,
'Ascanione pater Romanas invidet arces?
'quid struit? aut qua spe inimica in gente moratur,
'nec prolem Ausoniam et Lavinia respicit arva?
'naviget: haec summa est; hic nostri nuntius esto.'

Vv. 238—278. *Mercury donning his winged sandals and taking his wand flies first to Atlas, thence plunges to the sea, and reaches Carthage, where he finds Aeneas gorgeously apparelled, superintending the buildings of Carthage. He delivers his message and departs.*

Dixerat. ille patris magni parere parabat
imperio: et primum pedibus talaria nectit
aurea, quae sublimem alis sive aequora supra
seu terram rapido pariter cum flamine portant.
tum virgam capit; hac animas ille evocat Orco
pallentes, alias sub Tartara tristia mittit;
dat somnos adimitque, et lumina morte resignat;
illa fretus agit ventos, et turbida tranat
nubila. iamque volans apicem et latera ardua cernit
Atlantis duri, caelum qui vertice fulcit,
Atlantis, cinctum adsidue cui nubibus atris
piniferum caput et vento pulsatur et imbri;
nix umeros infusa tegit: tum flumina mento
praecipitant senis, et glacie riget horrida barba.
hic primum paribus nitens Cyllenius alis

constitit; hinc toto praeceps se corpore ad undas
misit, avi similis, quae circum litora, circum
piscosos scopulos, humilis volat aequora iuxta.
haud aliter terras inter caelumque volabat
litus arenosum [ad] Libyae ventosque secabat
materno veniens ab avo Cyllenia proles.
ut primum alatis tetigit magalia plantis,
Aenean fundantem arces ac tecta novantem
conspicit: atque illi stellatus iaspide fulva
ensis erat, Tyrioque ardebat murice laena,
demissa ex umeris, dives quae munera Dido
fecerat et tenui telas discreverat auro.
continuo invadit: 'tu nunc Carthaginis altae
'fundamenta locas, pulchramque uxorius urbem
'exstruis, heu regni rerumque oblite tuarum?
'ipse deum tibi me claro demittit Olympo
'regnator, caelum et terras qui numine torquet;
'ipse haec ferre iubet celeres mandata per auras:
'quid struis? aut qua spe Libycis teris otia terris?
'si te nulla movet tantarum gloria rerum,
'nec super ipse tua moliris laude laborem,
'Ascanium surgentem et spes heredis Iuli
'respice, cui regnum Italiae Romanaque tellus
'debentur.' tali Cyllenius ore locutus
mortales visus medio sermone reliquit,
et procul in tenuem ex oculis evanuit auram.

Vv. 279—295. *Aeneas, horror-struck at the vision, and the words of the god, rapidly makes up his mind, passes the word to his chieftains to make ready for instant departure, and to give no reason for their movements. He meanwhile must break the news to Dido.*

At vero Aeneas aspectu obmutuit amens,
arrectaeque horrore comae, et vox faucibus haesit.
ardet abire fuga, dulcesque relinquere terras,
attonitus tanto monitu imperioque deorum.
heu, quid agat? quo nunc reginam ambire furentem
audeat adfatu? quae prima exordia sumat?
atque animum nunc huc celerem, nunc dividit illuc,
in partesque rapit varias, perque omnia versat.
haec alternanti potior sententia visa est:
Mnesthea Sergestumque vocat, fortemque Serestum:
classem aptent taciti, sociosque ad litora cogant;
arma parent, et, quae rebus sit causa novandis,
dissimulent: sese interea, quando optima Dido
nesciat, et tantos rumpi non speret amores,
temptaturum aditus, et quae mollissima fandi
tempora, quis rebus dexter modus. ocius omnes
imperio laeti parent, ac iussa facessunt.

Vv. 296—330. *But she with the infallible instinct of love had scented danger in the air, even before Rumour brought her news of the preparations for sailing. Then distracted with passion, she seeks Aeneas, taunts him with trying to steal away at a season when nothing but a most urgent cause would induce a man to sail. 'Was she the cause? by all the love between them, by all the sacrifices she has made for his sake, she implores him to stay, and not leave her to die, friendless, without even a child to remember him by.'*

At regina dolos (quis fallere possit amantem?)
praesensit, motusque excepit prima futuros,

omnia tuta timens. eadem impia Fama furenti
detulit armari classem cursumque parari.
saevit inops animi, totamque incensa per urbem
bacchatur; qualis commotis excita sacris
Thyias, ubi audito stimulant trieterica Baccho
orgia, nocturnusque vocat clamore Cithaeron.
tandem his Aenean compellat vocibus ultro:
'dissimulare etiam sperasti, perfide, tantum
'posse nefas, tacitusque mea decedere terra?
'nec te noster amor, nec te data dextera quondam,
'nec moritura tenet crudeli funere Dido?
'quin etiam hiberno moliris sidere classem,
'et mediis properas Aquilonibus ire per altum,
'crudelis? quid? si non arva aliena domosque
'ignotas peteres, et Troia antiqua maneret,
'Troia per undosum peteretur classibus aequor?
'mene fugis? per ego has lacrimas dextramque tuam te,—
'quando aliud mihi iam miserae nihil ipsa reliqui—
'per conubia nostra, per inceptos hymenaeos,
'si bene quid de te merui, fuit aut tibi quidquam
'dulce meum: miserere domus labentis, et istam,
'oro, si quis adhuc precibus locus, exue mentem.
'te propter Libycae gentes Nomadumque tyranni
'odere, infensi Tyrii; te propter eundem
'exstinctus pudor, et, qua sola sidera adibam,
'fama prior. cui me moribundam deseris, hospes?
'hoc solum nomen quoniam de coniuge restat.
'quid moror? an mea Pygmalion dum moenia frater

'destruat, aut captam ducat Gaetulus Iarbas?
'saltem si qua mihi de te suscepta fuisset
'ante fugam suboles, si quis mihi parvulus aula
'luderet Aeneas, qui te tamen ore referret,
'non equidem omnino capta ac deserta viderer.'

Vv. 331—361. *Aeneas with the warning of Jupiter fresh in his mind suppresses his feelings, and in reply acknowledges his obligations to Dido which he will never forget, but denies any intention of secret flight. 'He never considered himself to be married to her. He had never meant to stay there. He would have returned to Troy if fate had permitted. As it was, the Gods and his duty to his father and son required him to make for Italy. Even now the messenger of the Gods had been sent in visible form to remind him of his duty.'*

Dixerat. ille Iovis monitis immota tenebat
lumina, et obnixus curam sub corde premebat.
tandem pauca refert: 'ego te, quae plurima fando
'enumerare vales, numquam, regina, negabo
'promeritam; nec me meminisse pigebit Elissae,
'dum memor ipse mei, dum spiritus hos regit artus.
'pro re pauca loquar. neque ego hanc abscondere furto
'speravi, ne finge, fugam; nec coniugis umquam
'praetendi taedas, aut haec in foedera veni.
'me si fata meis paterentur ducere vitam
'auspiciis, et sponte mea componere curas,
'urbem Troianam primum dulcesque meorum
'reliquias colerem; Priami tecta alta manerent,
'et recidiva manu posuissem Pergama victis.

'sed nunc Italiam magnam Gryneus Apollo,
'Italiam Lyciae iussere capessere sortes.
'hic amor, haec patria est. si te Carthaginis arces,
'Phoenissam, Libycaeque aspectus detinet urbis,
'quae tandem, Ausonia Teucros considere terra,
'invidia est? et nos fas extera quaerere regna.
'me patris Anchisae, quotiens umentibus umbris
'nox operit terras, quotiens astra ignea surgunt,
'admonet in somnis et turbida terret imago;
'me puer Ascanius, capitisque iniuria cari,
'quem regno Hesperiae fraudo et fatalibus arvis.
'nunc etiam interpres divom, Iove missus ab ipso,
'(testor utrumque caput) celeres mandata per auras
'detulit. ipse deum manifesto in lumine vidi
'intrantem muros, vocemque his auribus hausi.
'desine meque tuis incendere teque querellis;
'Italiam non sponte sequor.'

Vv. 362—392. *Dido replies with passionate reproaches, accusing him of faithlessness, cruelty and ingratitude. The divine mission was only an excuse. It began to be pressing because he wanted to get away from her, but she will follow him, and haunt him.*

Talia dicentem iamdudum aversa tuetur,
huc illuc volvens oculos, totumque pererrat
luminibus tacitis, et sic accensa profatur:
'nec tibi diva parens, generis nec Dardanus auctor,
'perfide; sed duris genuit te cautibus horrens
'Caucasus, Hyrcanaeque admorunt ubera tigres.
'nam quid dissimulo? aut quae me ad maiora reservo?

'num fletu ingemuit nostro? num lumina flexit?
'num lacrimas victus dedit, aut miseratus amantem
est?
'quae quibus anteferam? iam iam nec maxima Iuno,
'nec Saturnius haec oculis pater aspicit aequis.
'nusquam tuta fides. eiectum litore, egentem
'excepi, et regni demens in parte locavi;
'amissam classem, socios a morte reduxi.
'heu furiis incensa feror! nunc augur Apollo,
'nunc Lyciae sortes, nunc et Iove missus ab ipso
'interpres divom fert horrida iussa per auras.
'scilicet is superis labor est, ea cura quietos
'sollicitat. neque te teneo, neque dicta refello.
'i, sequere Italiam ventis; pete regna per undas.
'spero equidem mediis, si quid pia numina possunt,
'supplicia hausurum scopulis, et nomine Dido
'saepe vocaturum. sequar atris ignibus absens;
'et cum frigida mors anima seduxerit artus
'omnibus umbra locis adero. dabis, improbe, poenas;
'audiam, et haec manes veniet mihi fama sub imos.'
his medium dictis sermonem abrumpit, et auras
aegra fugit, seque ex oculis avertit et aufert,
linquens multa metu cunctantem et multa parantem
dicere. suscipiunt famulae, conlapsaque membra
marmoreo referunt thalamo stratisque reponunt.

Vv. 393—407. *Deeply grieved, Aeneas nevertheless carries out the divine command. The preparations are hurried on. The men and their movements are compared to ants at work.*

At pius Aeneas, quamquam lenire dolentem
solando cupit et dictis avertère curas,
multa gemens, magnoque animum labefactus amore,
iussa tamen divom exsequitur, classemque revisit.
tum vero Teucri incumbunt, et litore celsas
deducunt toto naves. natat uncta carina;
frondentesque ferunt remos et robora silvis
infabricata, fugae studio.
migrantes cernas, totaque ex urbe ruentes;
ac velut ingentem formicae farris acervom
cum populant, hiemis memores, tectoque reponunt:
it nigrum campis agmen, praedamque per herbas
convectant calle angusto; pars grandia trudunt
obnixae frumenta umeris; pars agmina cogunt
castigantque moras; opere omnis semita fervet.

Vv. 408—436. *Dido seeing them, and broken down by love, begs her sister to make one more appeal on her behalf to Aeneas. 'She does not ask him to stay as her husband, but only for a little while, till she can get accustomed to her new trouble. If she were an enemy, he could not treat her more harshly than he was doing. She had been a friend to him: let him grant her this little boon.'*

Quis tibi tum, Dido, cernenti talia sensus,
quosve dabas gemitus, cum litora fervere late
prospiceres arce ex summa, totumque videres
misceri ante oculos tantis clamoribus aequor?
improbe amor, quid non mortalia pectora cogis?
ire iterum in lacrimas, iterum temptare precando
cogitur, et supplex animos submittere amori,

ne quid inexpertum frustra moritura relinquat.
'Anna, vides toto properari litore: circum
'undique convenere; vocat iam carbasus auras,
'puppibus et laeti nautae inposuere coronas.
'hunc ego si potui tantum sperare dolorem,
'et perferre, soror, potero. miserae hoc tamen unum
'exsequere, Anna, mihi; solam nam perfidus ille
'te colere, arcanos etiam tibi credere sensus;
'sola viri molles aditus et tempora noras.
'i, soror, atque hostem supplex adfare superbum:
'non ego cum Danais Troianam exscindere gentem
'Aulide iuravi, classemve ad Pergama misi:
'nec patris Anchisae cinerem manesve revelli,
'cur mea dicta neget duras demittere in aures.
'quo ruit? extremum hoc miserae det munus amanti:
'exspectet facilemque fugam ventosque ferentes.
'non iam coniugium antiquum, quod prodidit, oro,
'nec pulchro ut Latio careat regnumque relinquat:
'tempus inane peto, requiem spatiumque furori,
'dum mea me victam doceat fortuna dolere.
'extremam hanc oro veniam,—miserere sororis;
'quam mihi cum dederis, cumulatam morte remittam.'

Vv. 437—449. *But Aeneas is not to be moved from his purpose. Like an oak he feels the force of the tempest and shows that he feels it, but does not yield to it.*

Talibus orabat, talesque miserrima fletus
fertque refertque soror. sed nullis ille movetur
fletibus, aut voces ullas tractabilis audit;

fata obstant, placidasque viri deus obstruit aures.
ac velut annoso validam cum robore quercum
Alpini Boreae nunc hinc nunc flatibus illinc
eruere inter se certant; it stridor, et alte
consternunt terram concusso stipite frondes:
ipsa haeret scopulis, et, quantum vertice ad auras
aetherias, tantum radice in Tartara tendit:
haud secus adsiduis hinc atque hinc vocibus heros
tunditur, et magno persentit pectore curas:
mens immota manet; lacrimae volvuntur inanes.

Vv. 450—473. *Then Dido prays for death. Evil omens, old prophecies recurring to her mind, and horrible dreams combine to drive her to suicide.*

Tum vero infelix fatis exterrita Dido
mortem orat; taedet caeli convexa tueri.
quo magis inceptum peragat, lucemque relinquat,
vidit, turicremis cum dona inponeret aris,
horrendum dictu, latices nigrescere sacros,
fusaque in obscenum se vertere vina cruorem.
hoc visum nulli, non ipsi effata sorori.
praeterea fuit in tectis de marmore templum
coniugis antiqui, miro quod honore colebat,
velleribus niveis et festa fronde revinctum:
hinc exaudiri voces et verba vocantis
visa viri, nox cum terras obscura teneret:
solaque culminibus ferali carmine bubo
saepe queri, et longas in fletum ducere voces.
multaque praeterea vatum praedicta piorum

terribili monitu horrificant. agit ipse furentem
in somnis ferus Aeneas; semperque relinqui
sola sibi, semper longam incomitata videtur
ire viam, et Tyrios deserta quaerere terra.
Eumenidum veluti demens videt agmina Pentheus,
et solem geminum, et duplices se ostendere Thebas;
aut Agamemnonius scaenis agitatus Orestes
armatam facibus matrem et serpentibus atris
cum fugit, ultricesque sedent in limine Dirae.

Vv. 474—503. *All that remains is to find fit time and means to carry out her purpose. For this she requires her sister's aid. This she obtains by telling her of a magic rite, learnt from a Massylian woman, which is to bring back Aeneas, or cure her of her love. To perform this charm it is necessary to burn the relics of Aeneas on a funeral pile. Anna unsuspecting carries out her sister's orders.*

Ergo ubi concepit furias evicta dolore
decrevitque mori, tempus secum ipsa modumque
exigit, et maestam dictis adgressa sororem
consilium voltu tegit, ac spem fronte serenat
'inveni, germana, viam—gratare sorori—
'quae mihi reddat eum, vel eo me solvat amantem.
'oceani finem iuxta solemque cadentem
'ultimus Aethiopum locus est, ubi maximus Atlas
'axem umero torquet stellis ardentibus aptum:
'hinc mihi Massylae gentis monstrata sacerdos,
'Hesperidum templi custos, epulasque draconi
'quae dabat, et sacros servabat in arbore ramos,
'spargens umida mella soporiferumque papaver.

'haec se carminibus promittit solvere mentes,
'quas velit, ast aliis duras inmittere curas;
'sistere aquam fluviis, et vertere sidera retro;
'nocturnosque ciet manes; mugire videbis
'sub pedibus terram, et descendere montibus ornos.
'testor, cara, deos, et te, germana, tuumque
'dulce caput, magicas invitam accingier artes.
'tu secreta pyram tecto interiore sub auras
'erige, et arma viri, thalamo quae fixa reliquit
'impius, exuviasque omnes, lectumque iugalem,
'quo perii, superinponant: abolere nefandi
'cuncta viri monimenta iuvat monstratque sacerdos.'
haec effata silet; pallor simul occupat ora.
non tamen Anna novis praetexere funera sacris
germanam credit, nec tantos mente furores
concipit, aut graviora timet, quam morte Sychaei.
ergo iussa parat.

Vv. 504–521. *The pile raised, and the relics placed on it, the priestess invokes the Gods, and scatters her charms. Dido at the altar makes a dying appeal to the Gods.*

At regina, pyra penetrali in sede sub auras
erecta, ingenti taedis atque ilice secta,
intenditque locum sertis, et fronde coronat
funerea; super exuvias ensemque relictum
effigiemque toro locat, haud ignara futuri.
stant arae circum, et crines effusa sacerdos
ter centum tonat ore deos, Erebumque Chaosque
tergeminamque Hecaten, tria virginis ora Dianae.

sparserat et latices simulatos fontis Averni;
falcibus et messae ad lunam quaeruntur aenis
pubentes herbae, nigri cum lacte veneni;
quaeritur et nascentis equi de fronte revolsus
et matri praereptus amor.
ipsa mola manibusque piis altaria iuxta,
unum exuta pedem vinclis, in veste recincta,
testatur moritura deos et conscia fati
sidera; tum, si quod non aequo foedere amantes
curae numen habet iustumque memorque, precatur.

Vv. 522—553. *Night comes on bringing rest to all creation, except to Dido. Sleepless and tossed by the tempest of her passion she communes with herself. 'She cannot seek aid from her rejected suitors, she cannot fly with the Trojans, she cannot bring Aeneas back by force. She must die. If only her sister had not encouraged her love! If only she might have never known what love meant!'*

Nox erat, et placidum carpebant fessa soporem
corpora per terras, silvaeque et saeva quierant
aequora, cum medio volvuntur sidera lapsu,
cum tacet omnis ager, pecudes, pictaeque volucres,
quaeque lacus late liquidos, quaeque aspera dumis
rura tenent, somno positae sub nocte silenti
lenibant curas, et corda oblita laborum.
at non infelix animi Phoenissa, neque umquam
solvitur in somnos, oculisve aut pectore noctem
accipit: ingeminant curae, rursusque resurgens
saevit amor, magnoque irarum fluctuat aestu.
sic adeo insistit, secumque ita corde volutat:

'en, quid ago? rursusne procos inrisa priores
'experiar, Nomadumque petam conubia supplex,
'quos ego sim totiens iam dedignata maritos?
'Iliacas igitur classes atque ultima Teucrum
'iussa sequar? quiane auxilio iuvat ante levatos,
'et bene apud memores veteris stat gratia facti?
'quis me autem, fac velle, sinet, ratibusve superbis
'invisam accipiet? nescis heu, perdita, necdum
'Laomedonteae sentis periuria gentis?
'quid tum? sola fuga nautas comitabor ovantes?
'an Tyriis omnique manu stipata meorum
'inferar, et, quos Sidonia vix urbe revelli,
'rursus agam pelago, et ventis dare vela iubebo?
'quin morere, ut merita es, ferroque averte dolorem.
'tu lacrimis evicta meis, tu prima furentem
'his, germana, malis oneras, atque obicis hosti.
'non licuit thalami expertem sine crimine vitam
'degere, more ferae, tales nec tangere curas!
'non servata fides, cineri promissa Sychaeo!'
tantos illa suo rumpebat pectore questus.

Vv. 554—583. *Aeneas sleeping on board his ship, is warned by Mercury in a dream to sail away at once, or Dido would attack him and set fire to his fleet. Aeneas at once rouses his men, and they put to sea immediately.*

Aeneas celsa in puppi, iam certus eundi,
carpebat somnos, rebus iam rite paratis.
huic se forma dei voltu redeuntis eodem
obtulit in somnis, rursusque ita visa monere est,
omnia Mercurio similis, vocemque coloremque

et crines flavos et membra decora iuventa:
'nate dea, potes hoc sub casu ducere somnos?
'nec, quae te circum stent deinde pericula, cernis,
'demens, nec Zephyros audis spirare secundos?
'illa dolos dirumque nefas in pectore versat,
'certa mori, variosque irarum concitat aestus.
'non fugis hinc praeceps, dum praecipitare potestas?
'iam mare turbari trabibus, saevasque videbis
'conlucere faces, iam fervere litora flammis,
'si te his attigerit terris Aurora morantem.
'heia age, rumpe moras. varium et mutabile semper
'femina.' sic fatus nocti se immiscuit atrae.
tum vero Aeneas subitis exterritus umbris
corripit e somno corpus, sociosque fatigat:
'praecipites vigilate, viri, et considite transtris;
'solvite vela citi. deus aethere missus ab alto
'festinare fugam tortosque incidere funes
'ecce iterum instimulat. sequimur te, sancte deorum,
'quisquis es, imperioque iterum paremus ovantes.
'adsis o placidusque iuves, et sidera caelo
'dextra feras.' dixit, vaginaque eripit ensem
fulmineum, strictoque ferit retinacula ferro.
idem omnes simul ardor habet; rapiuntque ruuntque:
litora deseruere; latet sub classibus aequor;
adnixi torquent spumas et caerula verrunt.

Vv. 584—629. *At dawn Dido looking forth sees the fleet sailing away. Then she fully realises her loss, and breaks out into impotent fury, savagely regretting her kind forbearance towards Aeneas. She prays to the Gods to load him with misfortunes, and to put eternal hostility between her people and his.*

Et iam prima novo spargebat lumine terras
Tithoni croceum linquens Aurora cubile.
regina e speculis ut primum albescere lucem
vidit, et aequatis classem procedere velis,
litoraque et vacuos sensit sine remige portus,
terque quaterque manu pectus percussa decorum
flaventesque abscissa comas, 'pro Iuppiter! ibit
'hic,' ait, 'et nostris inluserit advena regnis?
'non arma expedient, totaque ex urbe sequentur,
'deripientque rates alii navalibus? ite,
'ferte citi flammas, date vela, inpellite remos.
'quid loquor? aut ubi sum? quae mentem insania mutat?
'infelix Dido! nunc te facta impia tangunt?
'tum decuit, cum sceptra dabas. en dextra fidesque,
'quem secum patrios aiunt portare penates,
'quem subiisse umeris confectum aetate parentem!
'non potui abreptum divellere corpus, et undis
'spargere? non socios, non ipsum absumere ferro
'Ascanium, patriisque epulandum ponere mensis?
'verum anceps pugnae fuerat fortuna.—fuisset;
'quem metui moritura? faces in castra tulissem,
'implessemque foros flammis, natumque patremque
'cum genere exstinxem, memet super ipsa dedissem.
'sol, qui terrarum flammis opera omnia lustras,
'tuque harum interpres curarum et conscia Iuno,
'nocturnisque Hecate triviis ululata per urbes,

'et Dirae ultrices, et di morientis Elissae,
'accipite haec, meritumque malis advertite numen,
'et nostras audite preces. si tangere portus
'infandum caput ac terris adnare necesse est,
'et sic fata Iovis poscunt, hic terminus haeret:
'at bello audacis populi vexatus et armis,
'finibus extorris, complexu avolsus Iuli,
'auxilium inploret, videatque indigna suorum
'funera; nec, cum se sub leges pacis iniquae
'tradiderit, regno aut optata luce fruatur,
'sed cadat ante diem mediaque inhumatus arena.
'haec precor; hanc vocem extremam cum sanguine fundo.
'tum vos, o Tyrii, stirpem et genus omne futurum
'exercete odiis, cinerique haec mittite nostro
'munera. nullus amor populis, nec foedera sunto.
'exoriare aliquis nostris ex ossibus ultor,
'qui face Dardanios ferroque sequare colonos,
'nunc, olim, quocumque dabunt se tempore vires.
'litora litoribus contraria, fluctibus undas
'inprecor, arma armis; pugnent ipsique nepotesque.'

Vv. 630—662. *Then determined to die she sends away Sychaeus' nurse with orders to bring her sister to complete the magic ceremony. In the absence of the nurse she mounts the pile and after a few words, claiming credit for what she has done and compassionating her own wretched end, stabs herself with Aeneas' sword.*

Haec ait, et partes animum versabat in omnes,
invisam quaerens quam primum abrumpere lucem.

tum breviter Barcen nutricem adfata Sychaei;
namque suam patria antiqua cinis ater habebat:
'Annam cara mihi nutrix huc siste sororem;
'dic, corpus properet fluviali spargere lympha,
'et pecudes secum et monstrata piacula ducat:
'sic veniat, tuque ipsa pia tege tempora vitta.
'sacra Iovi Stygio, quae rite incepta paravi,
'perficere est animus, finemque inponere curis;
'Dardaniique rogum capitis permittere flammae.'
sic ait. illa gradum studio celerabat anili.
at trepida et coeptis immanibus effera Dido,
sanguineam volvens aciem, maculisque trementes
interfusa genas, et pallida morte futura,
interiora domus inrumpit limina, et altos
conscendit furibunda rogos, ensemque recludit
Dardanium, non hos quaesitum munus in usus.
hic postquam Iliacas vestes notumque cubile
conspexit, paulum lacrimis et mente morata,
incubuitque toro, dixitque novissima verba:
'dulces exuviae, dum fata deusque sinebant,
'accipite hanc animam, meque his exsolvite curis.
'vixi, et, quem dederat cursum fortuna, peregi;
'et nunc magna mei sub terras ibit imago.
'urbem praeclaram statui; mea moenia vidi:
'ulta virum, poenas inimico a fratre recepi:
'felix, heu nimium felix, si litora tantum
'numquam Dardaniae tetigissent nostra carinae!'
dixit: et os inpressa toro, 'moriemur inultae,
'sed moriamur,' ait. 'sic, sic iuvat ire sub umbras.

'hauriat hunc oculis ignem crudelis ab alto
'Dardanus, et nostrae secum ferat omina mortis.'

Vv. 663—705. *Her attendants at once raise an alarm, which spreads through the city. Anna hearing it, rushes to the spot, and with bitter lamentation over the deception she has allowed to be practised on her, mounts the pyre. There the queen lies struggling to die. But because she was perishing prematurely and by her own hand and* Proserpina *had not yet consecrated her to the Gods below, she could not die. Juno in pity sends Iris to perform the office of consecration and release the queen's soul.*

Dixerat: atque illam media inter talia ferro
conlapsam aspiciunt comites, ensemque cruore
spumantem, sparsasque manus. it clamor ad alta
atria; concussam bacchatur Fama per urbem.
lamentis gemituque et femineo ululatu
tecta fremunt; resonat magnis plangoribus aether.
non aliter quam si inmissis ruat hostibus omnis
Carthago, aut antiqua Tyros, flammaeque furentes
culmina perque hominum volvantur perque deorum.
audiit exanimis, trepidoque exterrita cursu
unguibus ora soror foedans et pectora pugnis
per medios ruit, ac morientem nomine clamat:
'hoc illud, germana, fuit? me fraude petebas?
'hoc rogus iste mihi, hoc ignes araeque parabant?
'quid primum deserta querar? comitemne sororem
'sprevisti moriens? eadem me ad fata vocasses:
'idem ambas ferro dolor, atque eadem hora tulisset.
'his etiam struxi manibus, patriosque vocavi

'voce deos, sic te ut posita crudelis abessem?
'exstinxti te meque, soror, populumque patresque
'Sidonios, urbemque tuam. date volnera lymphis
'abluam, et extremus si quis super halitus errat,
'ore legam.' sic fata gradus evaserat altos,
semianimemque sinu germanam amplexa fovebat
cum gemitu, atque atros siccabat veste cruores.
illa, graves oculos conata attollere, rursus
deficit; infixum stridit sub pectore volnus.
ter sese attollens cubitoque adnixa levavit:
ter revoluta toro est, oculisque errantibus alto
quaesivit caelo lucem, ingemuitque reperta.
tum Iuno omnipotens, longum miserata dolorem
difficilesque obitus, Irim demisit Olympo,
quae luctantem animam nexosque resolveret artus.
nam, quia nec fato merita nec morte peribat,
sed misera ante diem, subitoque accensa furore,
nondum illi flavom Proserpina vertice crinem
abstulerat, Stygioque caput damnaverat Orco.
ergo Iris croceis per caelum roscida pennis,
mille trahens varios adverso sole colores,
devolat, et supra caput adstitit: 'hunc ego Diti
'sacrum iussa fero, teque isto corpore solvo.'
sic ait, et dextra crinem secat. omnis et una
dilapsus calor, atque in ventos vita recessit.

NOTES.

2. **venis**] abl. of instr. 'with her life-blood.'

caeco] a use of the adj. in which persons and things are identified with their attributes or circumstances. Dido blind to the passion which is wearing her is said to be consumed by a blind flame of love. So *tarda podagra*, where the adj., as often in these cases, practically acquires a transitive force.

3. **multa**] 'The worth courses back (so as to be) many'= 'The worth courses back often.' *multa* is part of the pred. and practically = an adv.

6. **lustrabat**] Con. says there is no authority for taking *lustro* = *illustro*; and he is probably right. But there can be little doubt that Vergil meant to suggest that meaning as well as the usual one of 'traverse.' V. often adds fulness to his language by using words which suggest more than they actually express.

11. **quem &c.**] *se fero*, like our words 'bearing,' 'carriage,' 'presence,' implies dignity of bearing; 'bearing himself what a man!' therefore means 'what a majesty is in his mien!' The Graecising use of the interrog. pron. in a participial clause should be noticed.

armis] It is a question whether this comes from *armus* or *arma*, and there is much to be said on both sides. On the whole I agree with Kv. that it comes from *arma*, not because the other is coarse or unpoetical, but because (1) *armus* was regularly used of animals (as Ovid, Met. x. 700, shows, where, speaking of the transformation of human beings into lions, he has *ex humeris* armi *fiunt*); and Vergil was not likely to use it in an ambiguous case of a man's shoulders without some explanatory word to show his meaning: (2) if taken from *arma* and understood (as also *pectore*) in a metaphorical sense, 'what a gallant heart! what prowess!' it connects the line naturally with v. 13. Aeneas' gallantry proves his lineage because fear betrays the unheroic man.

12. **nec vana fides**] sc. *est.*

13. **degeneres**] generally means 'degenerate.' Here it clearly means 'unheroic.' The fact is Vergil gives the word an arbitrary but etymological meaning, trusting to the context to make it clear. 'Unpedigreed' men are those who cannot claim descent from the gods, i.e. are not heroes.

quibus...quae] the double interrogative in one sentence (Greek form) should be noticed.

16. **ne**] expresses the *purpose* implied in *animo sederet.*

17. **morte**] sc. *sua*, 'died to cheat me and frustrate my hopes'; a self-compassionate way of expressing the death of her husband Sychaeus, killed by Dido's brother Pygmalion.

19. **potui**] vivid use of the indicative instead of subj. in conditional sentence. 'I *had* found it in me,' instead of '*should have* found it in me.' So Georg. II. 133, *si non alium late iactaret odorem, Laurus* erat. The indic. seems to imply that the thing was very near happening. But picturesqueness merely and metrical convenience also have something to say probably to the use in poetry.

21. **fraterna caede**] 'murder *by* a brother,' 'a brother's murderous hand,' cf. 17.

22. **labantem**] evidently proleptic, *impulit ut labaret*, 'staggered.'

24. **dehiscat**] oblique command without the usual connecting *ut*. So after *volo*, and more regularly after *velim* and *vellem*. *Musa velim memores, Velim hoc facias* &c.

27. **ante**] redundant, but added probably because of the distance of *prius* from *quam*.

violo] It is rather curious evidence of the present uncertainty as to the exact relation of subj. and indic., that Mr Sidgwick sees in the indic. here 'a more forcible rejection of the deed,' while Mr Papillon says that it 'indicates a presentiment that dishonour *is* coming.' Prof. Conington's note is obscure, as is Dr Kennedy's. The probability is that the *present* indic. implies neither the rejection of the deed implied in *resolvo*, nor the contemplation of it as probable, but simply states it abstractly, apart from Dido's feelings about it, as the event before which she wishes something to happen.

34. **manes sepultos**] hypallage = *manes sepulti.*

35. **esto**] concessive, vivid way of expressing *sane*.

36. **Libyae**] if the correct reading, is locative. Cf. III. 162 *Cretae*.

37. **triumphis**] an anachronism, or a prophetic allusion to the Roman triumphs which were to be won by successes in Africa.

38. **placito**] participle of *placet*, one of several perf. pass. participles of neuter verbs used in neuter sense, e.g. *solitus*, *cretus*.

40. **genus**] in apposition to the sense of 'people' implied in *urbes*.

41. **infreni**] therefore more formidable as they could use both arms freely as they rode.

42. **siti**] see Introd. 'the thirsty desert.'

lateque] 'the roving fiends of Barce.'

43. **Barcaei**] anachronism. Barce was founded considerably later.

49. **rebus**] abl. of attendant circumstance. 'How grandly shall Punic glory lift its head.'

50. **litatis**] originally a neuter verb, 'to sacrifice with favorable omens,' 'to win the favor of the gods by sacrifice,' with dat. of the god and abl. of the thing sacrificed, is used later, as here, in act. sense with the acc. of the sacrifice. 'Anna assumes that the gods will be easy to reconcile.' Con.

51. **causas** &c.] 'Find [string] reason upon reason for delay,' lit. 'weave a string of delays.'

52. **pelago**] local abl. *desaevit* 'is spending (*de*) his rage.'

aquosus] either pred. 'brings rain' (Sidgwick), or attribute, in which case a verb must be supplied from *desaevit* to *Orion*. Both the rising (midsummer) and the setting (November) of Orion are spoken of as attended with storms. Ribbeck with considerable plausibility considers 52, 3 an interpolation: *dum quassatae rates* is very harsh, and *non tractabile caelum* a rather meaningless repetition.

55. **spem**] 'Dido's wishes were on one side, her scruples and fears on the other: Anna by removing her scruples allowed her to hope.' Con.

56. **pacem]** the 'leave' of the gods, as *pace tua* 'by your leave.' They sought an assurance that the gods would not be offended by what they were going to do.

59. All the gods here mentioned seem to have been connected with marriage. The difficulty is to see why *cui...curae* is added in the case of Juno. The difficulty might be removed by placing a comma at *Iunoni*, but the rhythm seems to forbid it.

63. **instaurat]** *instauro* means 'to renew,' either in the sense of doing the same thing over again, as in the technical sense of repeating a ceremony which has been wrongly performed, or in the sense of doing a similar thing, as in Cic. Verr. I. iv. *scelus illud pristinum renovavit et instauravit quaestorium.* Here *instaurare diem*='to begin a new day with similar gifts.'

64. **pectoribus]** the quantity is an archaism.

65. **heu &c.]** 'Oh! the blindness of seers!' If the soothsayers who assisted Dido had possessed any real insight they would have seen that their art was no use in her case. For the absolute use of *ignarus* cf. Sallust Cat. 51. 27 *ubi imperium ad ignaros aut minus bonos pervenit.*

67. **tacitum]** cf. 2.

69. **coniecta]** 'struck by a fatal arrow,' lit. 'an arrow having been shot so as to hit its mark.' For the sense of *coniecta* cf. IX. 698 *coniecto sternit iaculo.*

71. **agens]** used absolutely, as we use 'hunting'='hunting game.'

72. **nescius]** Aeneas corresponds to the shepherd, unconscious of the wound he has inflicted.

75. **urbem paratam]** 'is of course an appeal to the weariness of those whose city was yet to seek.' Con.

80. **lumen]** 'her own light.' *obscura*, proleptic, 'so as to be dark,' 'in darkness.'

82. **relictis]** i.e. by Aeneas.

83. **illum &c.]** The description of the night apparently ends at *incubat*. From *illum &c.* describes what Dido did at any time when Aeneas was away from her. The real difficulty of the passage lies in the nursing of a young gentleman old enough to hunt wild beasts.

88 **tuta]** 'safeguards in war.' The adj. is transitive, the

condition of the persons defended being transferred to the defences; cf. v. 2.

89. **machina**] Variously interpreted to mean 'scaffolding,' 'pile of building,' 'turret on the wall,' 'military engine,' and 'crane.' With the two last *cessat* or some similar word must be supplied from *pendent interrupta*.

90. **peste**] 'fatal passion,' so *pesti devota futurae* I. 712, also of Dido.

91. **cara**] Homer's φίλη ἄλοχος, used of Hera.

famam] 'care for her good name cannot curb her passion,' i.e. no human motive can save her.

96. **adeo**] used as a particle intensifying the word it follows. 'You cannot deceive *me*.' So Ecl. IV. 11 *Teque adeo decus hoc aevi* &c. 'In *thy* consulship &c.' Ecl. II. 25.

98. **certamine**] if right, depends on the sense of *quid opus est* implied in *quo*.

99. **pactosque hymenaeos**] the *que* adds a particular result of *pacem*.

100. **exercemus**] so *exercere amicitias*, *inimicitias* &c. The idea seems to be to bring something into shape by working at it.

101. **traxit**] 'has let the flame spread over all her frame.' The consequence of Dido's action is regarded as her own *action*. So Livy XXI. 8 *nec ullo pedem referente ne in locum a se relictum hostem inmitteret*. 'The notion in *traxit* is that of length or extension, the flame coursing through her bones.' Con.

102. **paribus**] 'with equal auspices,' = 'with equal sovereign rights.' The right of taking auspices belonging to the magistrates of the Roman State.

104. **dotalis**] 'as her dowry.'

105. **simulata**] her words were masked. She pretended one purpose and meant another.

106. **quo**] 'in order that,' in prose as a rule only used so with comparatives.

107. **demens**] is part of the predicate, 'who could regret like a madman,' so that the expression = *quis tam demens esset ut* &c.

109. **si modo**] i.e. the only feeling which could make one

hesitate to accept your proposal is doubt whether it could be carried out.

110. **fatis**] grammatically is probably governed by *feror*. But *incerta feror* together give the notion of blind uncertain wandering, so that in sense *fatis* is equal to an obj. gen. after *incerta feror*, in the neuter sense it frequently has 'to move quickly,' here with an accessory sense from the context of 'moving uncertainly,' 'wandering,' 'being all abroad.' 'About the will of the gods I have no light to guide me, whether &c.'

116. **confieri**] is unusual. The general rule is that prepositional compounds of *facio* keep the same form throughout.

119. **Titan**] the sun, as being son of the Titan, Hyperion.

121. **alae**] it seems best to take this as=*alatores*. But whether these were huntsmen or beaters is uncertain.

127. **hic**] either 'here' or 'this,' acc. as *Hymenaeus* is taken to mean 'marriage' or 'marriage-god.' The latter seems preferable.

128. **dolis**] probably (so Kv.) the scheme devised by Juno which promised congenial occupation to the goddess of love.

131. **rara**] 'large-meshed,' natural epithet of nets used in hunting large game.

'The distinction between *plaga* and *rete* is probably guesswork.' Kennedy. *plaga* is generally said to have been a smaller net used to bar roads, paths &c.

A verb must be supplied to these words from *ruunt* which applies properly to *equites* only. *lato ferro*, abl. of description.

132. **vis**] either means 'number,' as in Livy II. v. 3 *magna vis hominum immissa*, in which case *odora* is by hypallage for *odorarum*; or 'power' in which case the expression is an example of the form synecdoche by which a thing is described by an attribute, e.g. *mitis sapientia Laeli*, ='scenting power of dogs'='keen-scented dogs': *odorus* is not used elsewhere in the sense of 'having scent.'

133. **cunctantem**] expresses rather the impatient expectation of the chieftains than actual delay on the part of Dido.

137. **chlamydem**] This use of the acc. after passive verbs, especially the perf. pass. participle, is undoubtedly a Graecism, an imitation, that is, of the acc. after the middle (reflexive) voice (as here) or of the acc. after the passive voice. In the

latter case in Greek, the acc. is either cognate or governed by the *sense* of the passive verb. In *ἐπιτετραμμένος τὴν ἀρχήν* (instanced by Mr Sidgwick) *τὴν ἀρχήν* is the trust received (cognate), *χεῖρα βαρυνθεὶς* (cf. *pressus mentem* III. 47) is 'carrying or suffering a disabled hand.'

The chlamys was an oblong mantle fastened over the right shoulder or across the breast. It was specially used in riding.

picto limbo] is descriptive abl., cf. 131.

138. **in aurum**] is a forced expression for 'fastened into a knot with a golden pin.' The object is to pile the *aurum;* 'are shaped to a knot with gold.'

142. **iungit**] sc. *sibi*, 'heads the troops.' Or perhaps 'forms the link between the two troops,' Dido's and his own.

144. Apollo was supposed to migrate from Lycia in the summer and visit Delos, where worshippers from different countries assembled. Cretans were said to have been established by Apollo at Crisa as priests of his temple. Dryopes belonged to the neighbourhood of Parnassus. The Agathyrsi, who tattooed themselves (*picti*), belonged to Apollo's Hyperborean worshippers.

150. **tantum**] = *non minus.*

158. **votis**] dat. after *dari.*

160. **misceri**] a favourite word of Vergil's to suggest confused irregular disorderly movement physical or mental. XII. 444 *tum caeco pulvere campus* miscetur, 'a tumult of blinding dust.' I. 191 *omnem miscet agens telis turbam*, of the 'wild disorder' of the hunted deer. I. 134 *caelum terramque*...miscere, 'to confound earth and sky.' XII. 805 *luctu* miscere *hymenaeos*, 'to change a bridal to a scene of wild grief.' XII. 217 *vario* misceri *pectora motu*, of the agitation of conflicting feelings. Here the sky is represented as agitated by the thunder, 'the voice of thunder fills the troubled sky.'

166. **pronuba**] not so much a general epithet of Juno here, but describing her action on this occasion, 'acting as *pronuba*, bride-escorter.' The *pronuba* was a married woman who escorted the bride to the *lectus genialis*. The storm and the nymphs supply the other accompaniments of the wedding ceremony, the lightning representing the torches, with which the bride was conducted to her new home, the voices of the nymphs (the sounds of woods and waters) the hymeneal song.

170. **specie**] the appearance of her action, *fama*, what can be said of it. 'She cares nothing for the common eye or the common tongue.' Con.

175. **mobilitate**] is surely an abl. of cause: 'quick movement lends it vigour and it gathers strength as it goes.' Cf. Lucr. VI. 340 (a passage which probably suggested this) *mobilitatem...quae crescit eundo et validas auget vires* (sc. *suas*).

176. **primo**] is best taken as adv., or at any rate as an adverbial use of the adj., and *metu* as abl. of cause, 'small and shrinking at first.'

178. **ira**] because of the destruction of her offspring the Titans and the giants: *deorum*, objective, 'against the gods.'

180. **pernicibus**] qualifies both *pedibus* and *alis*.

181. **cui quot &c.**] 'for every feather on her body shows a wakeful eye beneath, a tongue, a voiceful mouth, a pricking ear.'

184. **medio**] substantival, 'in the space between.'

188. **tam ficti &c.**] 'reporting truth, but loving to deal with distorted fiction.'

191. **cretum**] cf. *placito* 38.

193. **quam longa**] 'all the winter long,' lit. during the winter, as long as it is.' Cf. VIII. 86 *Thybris ea fluvium, quam longa est, nocte tumentem leniit.*

195. **passim**] She first does her duty to the public, and as soon as that is finished (*protinus*) flies off to inflame Iarbas.

201. **excubias**] 'The gods' unsleeping sentry.' Con. The words are in loose apposition to *ignem*.

202. **solum** and **limina**] may be independent subjects to predicates *pingue* and *florentia*, or may depend on *sacraverat*.

203. **animi**] possibly a locative, as *me animi fallit* in Lucretius, but more probably (considering the similarity in meaning of *mens* and *animus*) a Graecising genitive, on the model of such expressions as *ἀρσένων παίδων ἄπαις*, where the gen. repeats the sense of the adjective and limits the application of it. Vergil's expression is near enough in sense to *impotens* or *inops animi* to justify the Graecism.

204. **numina**] 'In the sacred presence of the gods.' The expression is probably intended to suggest statues of the gods

in whose presence I. makes his appeal to Jupiter. It is possible that the right reading is *munera*, which would give a very good sense, 'amid his own gifts to the gods.'

205. **multa**] signifies the intensity rather than the length of his prayer. So πολύς is often used in Greek, e.g. πολὺς ἐνέκειτο, πόλλ' εὔχετο &c.

supinis] the regular position of the hands in prayer, with the palms up.

206. **nunc**] implies that Iarbas had introduced the Maurusian nation to the worship of Jupiter.

207. **epulata**] aorist use of the perf. partic., expressing the action of the verb as accompaniment of another action without reference to time, common with deponents, e.g. *ausus*, *perosus*, *imitatus* &c.

208—210. The important words in these sentences are *nequiquam*, *caeci* and *inania*. 'Is our awe of thee groundless, and the sights and sounds which inspire that awe meaningless?'

212. **pretio**] abl. of price, 'bought leave to build,' Con.

213. **leges**] 'jurisdiction.' 'Whom we have made queen of the spot.' Con.

215. **Paris**] used descriptively. Aeneas is called a second Paris, because he steals another man's bride.

217. **subnexus**] In spite of MS. authority in favour of *subnixus* it seems almost impossible to adopt it. The idea of a man having his chin propped with a ribbon is very far-fetched, and *mitra* suggests far more readily the cap or bonnet than the lappet with which it was fastened. *Subnexus* states that it was so fastened. The *mitra* was apparently a sort of turban worn by Greek women and Asiatic men.

218. **quippe**] in ironical sense, as frequently, qualifies *tuis* 'doubtless thine.' 'There *can* be no doubt that you dwell in these temples, because you never show your power to aid your worshippers.'

fovemus] 'hug to our hearts an empty name.'

225. **exspectat**] Vergil is peculiar in this use of *exspecto* without an object as = *moror*.

227. **talem**] = *talem fore*.

228. **ideo**] 'on the strength of her promise was able to rescue him.'

bis] 'can only refer to the two deliverances of Aeneas with which Venus is associated, that from Diomede (Il. v. 311 fol.) and that from the Greeks at the sack of Troy (Aen. II. 589 fol.).' Con.

229. **gravidam**] 'pregnant with empire and clamorous with war.' Sidgwick.

233. **super ipse sua**] The order is a Graecism, cf. Aesch. P.V. ἐπ' αὐτὸς αὑτῷ.

235. **spe**] Vergil's use of hiatus is prob. due to imitation of Homer, in whom it is generally apparent only, being due to omission of the digamma or *j* in writing. Vergil has it in the arsis of the foot after all the vowels except *u* and after the diphthong *æ* generally in the 3rd or 4th foot.

237. **hic**] adv. = *de hac re. Summa*, subst. The sum total, which is contained in *naviget*. 'This is my command in brief.'

240. **alis**] completes *sublimem*, 'raised by means of wings,' 'soaring.'

242. **virgam**] The staff (ῥάβδος, Gk.: *caduceus*, Lat.) which was one of the attributes of Hermes or Mercury. It was a combination in one of the herald's staff which he carried as messenger of the gods, and the magic wand with which he performed his different functions. *evocat* seems to be an extension of Mercury's functions; elsewhere he is represented only as conducting shades *to* Hades. *Orcus* and *Tartara* appear to be used here in a general sense for *Hades*.

244. **somnos**] So Homer Od. v. 47 τῇ τ' ἀνδρῶν ὄμματα θέλγει ὧν ἐθέλει τοὺς δ' αὖτε καὶ ὑπνώοντας ἐγείρει.

The whole of this description is modelled on the passage in which these lines occur.

resignat] The least unsatisfactory rendering of this seems to be to understand *resigno* = 'seal' or 'close,' and to regard the action as an extension of Mercury's sleep-giving function. The other explanations take *resigno* in the ordinary sense of 'unsealing,' so 'opening.' (1) 'Opens the eyes in (after) death,' referring to the custom of unclosing the eyes of a corpse when placed on the pyre, here attributed to Mercury as ψυχοπομπός to enable the dead to see their way. (2) 'Opens the eyes from death,' i.e. 'brings to life again.' The words from *hac animas* to *resignat* are parenthetical.

248. **Atlantis]** The giant who was fabled to support the sky is here identified with the African mountain of the same name.

256—258. The lines have been regarded as spurious with some reason. The MS. readings show some differences, the lines do not add anything to the simile but rather drag after it and *litus arenosum Libyae* is very difficult to construe. Conington renders *litus ventosque secabat*, 'he was dividing the shore from the winds,' 'he was flying close to the shore so as to be as it were between the winds and the shore.' But this would surely require *et* before *litus*. The *ad* found in some MSS. before *Libyae* seems not to be genuine. The best way to render the lines as they stand seems to be to take *litus ar. Lib.* as acc. after *volabat*, a sense-construction (or cognate acc.) like *currimus aequor*.

259. **magalia]** a Punic word, used here apparently for 'the suburb,' i.e. the smaller houses on the outskirts of the city as opposed to the larger buildings in the city itself. Acc. to Servius (on Aen. I. 272) the suburbs of Carthage were called *Magalia*.

262. **laena]** (Gk. χλαῖνα), a cloak, fastened with a *fibula*. It was an old Roman garment, made generally of thick woollen material, used as protection against the weather, or as a wrap in going to and from the *cena*. Like the χλαῖνα it is a common garment of heroes in poets. Under the empire it was a garment of various price acc. to the dye used, and the point here, as Conington says, is the Tyrian purple, the most expensive dye, and the golden thread, which made the garment luxurious.

266. **uxorius]** 'a woman's thrall,' Sidgwick.

269. **torquet]** as Conington says, probably combines the notions of physical movement and government.

274. **spes]** 'the hopes entertained by Iulus.' Conington and Kennedy both render, 'the hopes afforded by I.' But that is not to the point. What Mercury says is 'if you do not care for yourself, you have no right to disappoint your son and heir.'

283. **agat]** deliberative subj. The present is vivid construction for imperf.

289. **aptent]** imperat. in oratio obliq., again the vivid present instead of imperf.

291. **optima]** an epithet skilfully adapted to intensify Aeneas' difficulty who felt obliged to act so unkindly towards this 'kindest of friends.'

292. **speret]** cf. 419.

293. **quae...quis]** subj. mood of *sum* omitted as these are dependent questions.

mollissima] cf. 2 *caeco*. 'The softest moments' are the moments when Dido would be softest.

296. **possit]** 'who could (if he tried)?' Stronger than 'who can?'

297. **prima]** 'before any.'

298. **tuta]** 'Fearing even where there was no danger,' i.e. sensitively alive to the possibility of danger and therefore certain to know by instinct when it began to be.

eadem] It is a question whether this is fem. sing., 'the same who visited Iarbas,' or neut. pl., *eadem quae praesensit*, 'to confirm her forebodings.'

300. **animi]** obj. gen. after *inops=impotens*.

301. **commotis]** The statue and sacred emblems of the god were brought out of the temple and moved violently.

302. **trieterica]** the orgies of Bacchus celebrated every three years on Mt. Cithaeron, near Thebes.

308. **moritura]** Dido full of the idea that Aeneas' departure would be death to her assumes the same knowledge on his part.

309. **quin &c.]** The very fact of his starting in winter showed that his object was to get away from her at once, though he knew it would break her heart (*crudelis*). If it were not so, he would not be sailing away in search of a *new* home at a time of the year when under ordinary circumstances men would not cross the sea to reach their old home.

314. **mene]** *ne=nonne*. ''Tis I that hurry thee away, say I not right?'

per ego] cf. Ter. Andr. III. iii. 6 (537) *per te deos oro*. Livy XXIII. 9, 2 *Per ego te, fili, quaecumque iura liberos iungunt parentibus, precor*. So in Greek, e.g. *μή πρός σε γονάτων* τῆς τε νεογάμου κόρης, where, as here, the verb of entreaty is implied.

319. **si quis**] cf. 293.

322. **qua sola**] variously rendered 'which alone would have been enough to make me immortal had there been nothing else,' and 'which was my only title to immortality.' But if it is to be taken in a literal, objective sense, *sidera adire* would mean apotheosis rather than simple immortality. It seems better to take the words as metaphorical, 'by which alone my spirit soared.' My one source of spiritual pride, which alone made me conscious of my moral superiority to others. But there is a good deal to be said for Kv.'s proposal to alter *sola* into *solem et*, which would obviate the difficulty.

330. **capta**] cheated, betrayed. So II. 196 *captique dolis lacrimisque coactis*. *Capio* in this sense differs from *decipio* in that it always implies harm done to the person deceived. Lucr. IV. 16 *deceptaque non capiatur*, 'be beguiled but not to its hurt.'

332. **obnixus**] adverbial use of partic. 'with strong effort.'

334. **numquam negabo**] favorite Latin use of double negation instead of affirmation. 'Thy lips cannot express (detail) more claims upon my gratitude, O queen, than I will ever gladly acknowledge.'

337. **pro re**] 'to suit the case,' 'as the case requires,' or 'as circumstances allow.'

338. **ne finge**] 'deceive not thyself with such a thought.' *furto*, abl. of manner, almost = *furtim*.

339. **praetendi**] seems to combine the literal notion of 'holding out' and the figurative of 'pretend,' 'use as a disguise.' 'I never used the bridegroom's torch (the forms of wedlock) to colour my action.' *haec*, 'such,' i.e. *coniugalia*.

341. **auspiciis**] cf. 103. 'Did Fate allow me to plan the conduct of my life's campaign.' The metaphor here is from the consul as commander-in-chief.

sponte mea] = *meo arbitrio*.

componere &c.] 'to unravel the tangles of my destiny,' **Con.**

345. **Gryneus**] belonging to Grynium a city of Aeolis in Asia Minor, where there was a famous grove and temple of Apollo.

346. **Lyciae**] that is of Patara in Lycia, another famous seat of Apollo's worship. Cf. 143.

The oracular warning alluded to is not mentioned elsewhere.

347. **hic**] meaning *Italia*, is attracted according to the regular idiom into the case of the predicate. Cf. VI. 128 *Sed revocare gradus superasque evadere ad auras hoc opus* hic *labor est*.

350. **invidia**] lit. 'what ground for grudging is settling' &c. i.e. 'why grudge us the privilege of settling.'

354. **me**] a verb, e.g. *commovet*, must be supplied from the preceding sentence.

360. **incendere**] here simply 'to agitate,' 'distress.'

362. **iamdudum**] like *πάλαι*, depends on the context for the actual length of time expressed. Here the impatience of Dido is implied in the use of the word, as in Soph. Electr. 676, *θανόντ' Ὀρέστην νῦν τε καὶ πάλαι λέγω*, the surprise of the paedagogus is expressed at the question of Clytemnestra, which seems to show that she had not listened to his statement in 673.

364. **tacitis**] cf. 2. She was silent, her eyes expressive; so that the sense implied is much the same as 'with speaking eyes.'

365. Comp. Ecl. VIII. 33 fol.

368. **aut quae**] 'She asks why she should hide her feelings as if there were likely to be any greater occasion to call forth their full force.' Con.

369. **num &c.**] 'Have my tears wrung from him one sigh, one melting look?'

371. **quae**] 'what shall I put before what?' seems to mean 'What shall I say first, [what last?] when there is so much, and that so important?' Cf. Eur. Electr. 907. The next words are open to three renderings. (1) Jupiter and Juno no longer look on this world with equal eyes, i.e. they no longer act as impartial controllers of actions in the world. (2) They no longer look on this kingdom with favorable eyes, i.e. they have deserted Carthage. (3) They cannot look on such conduct as this of Aeneas favorably. This must go beyond their patience. The last seems to suit the sense of *iam iam* and the context best.

375. **classem**] a verb must be supplied from *a morte reduxi.*

376. **nunc**] emphatic all through. It is a repetition of Aeneas' words 345, 356. *Apollo, sortes*, some verb must be supplied from the sense of *fert iussa &c.* e.g. *intervenit.*

383. **hausurum**] = suffer to the full, metaphor from emptying a vessel. So ἀντλεῖν. 'drain the cup of retribution to the dregs.'

384. **absens**] that is, the thought of her as an avenging fury, will never leave him. *ignibus*, allusion to the torches carried by the Erinnyes or Furies.

386. **adero**] After death she will be able to haunt him as a visible phantom, not simply as a recollection.

389. **fugit**] 'like *caelum fugit*, Georg. III. 417. She abhors the open day and is rushing into the house.' Con.

392. **thalamo**] dat. poetical use = *ad* with acc. So *It clamor caelo &c.*

395. **animum**] cf. 137.

397. **incumbunt**] used absolutely without a completing dat.

litore] local abl.

402. **ac velut**] here as in Aen. II. 626 *ac* = not 'and as,' but 'even as.'

406. **obnixae**] cf. 332.

407. **moras**] abstract for concrete, 'delays' = 'delayers.'

411. **misceri**] cf. 160.

412. **quid**] *cogo* here has double acc. on the analogy of *doceo* &c.

414. **animos**] *animi* used of a single person implies *high spirit, pride.*

415. **frustra**] 'and die in vain,' lit. 'destined in that case' (if she left any means untried which might have saved her) 'to die in vain,' since her death would be needless.

418. **coronas**] Georg. I. 304. It seems to have been a custom to hang garlands on ships entering or leaving port. But, if this verse is not an interpolation here, Dido must use the words in a conventional sense simply to express the near

approaching departure of the ships. Vergil could hardly make pious Aeneas guilty of such bad taste as to exhibit signs of rejoicing under the circumstances.

419. **sperare**] wants something to explain it which V. has not given. There is nothing to show that Dido expected her grief. It is represented as a sudden shock.

420. **tamen**] i.e. though I am able to bear it, make one effort to save me.

423. **aditus...tempora**] cf. 293.

427. **revelli**] There was a story that Diomede had taken up the bones of Anchises.

428. **cur**]=*ut ob eam causam.*

433. **inane**] 'vacant (leisure) time.'

requiem] predicative, 'to be rest &c.,' 'to give my distracted heart respite till &c.'

436. The different readings in these lines are *dederit* for *dederis*, *cumulata* for *cumulatam*, and *relinquam* for *remittam*. *Miserere sororis* seems to point to *dederis* as the right reading, and *cumulata morte* is not intelligible. *Remittam* is a difficulty in the sense of *reddam*; but *relinquam* (bequeath) is pretty obviously a correction suggested by *morte* and would fix the meaning of *morte*, which is just what Vergil did not mean to do. For the abl. would convey the idea of time or means according as the hearer was prepared to receive it. In fact it would mean one thing to Dido and another to Anna. The difficulty of translating it, lies in the necessity for a preposition which fixes it to one meaning. 'Grant me this boon and my death shall return it to thee with interest.'

438. **fertque refertque**] 'carries more than once from Dido,' adds force to the words that follow.

nullis]=*non aut ullis.* So that *aut* before *voces*=*nec.*

440. **placidas**] the general characteristic of the man, here cancelled for the time being by the action of the god.

449. **lacrimae**] probably Dido's are meant.

451. **orat**] either (1) 'makes her prayer to Death,' with which personification cf. Soph. Aj. 840, or (2) prays for death.

452. **quo magis**] that is to make her the more disposed to carry out her purpose.

459. **revinctum**] probably acc. agreeing with *quod*, and expressing part of the honour paid to the shrine by Dido.

464. **piorum**] there seems to be about equal MS. authority for this and *priorum*, but *piorum* sounds best. But the sense is probably the same with either. It was old prophecies forgotten till now which combined with portents and visions to terrify Dido.

469. Pentheus, king of Thebes, in punishment for forbidding the worship of Dionysus was torn in pieces by his mother Agave and her bacchantes. In the Bacchae of Euripides he is represented as inspired by Dionysus, who is leading him out to meet his death, with delusion, under which he sees 'two suns and two cities of Thebes.' His vision of the Eumenides Vergil drew from some other source, unless it is simply added as a conventional expression for a sudden access of insanity.

471. **scaenis**] loc. abl. 'hunted over the stage' by his mother and the Furies who come to avenge her murder. Clytemnestra is here represented as habited like a Fury herself. Vergil may have been thinking of the Eumenides of Aeschylus or of some Roman play on the same subject.

474. **concepit**] 'shaped' or 'formed.' Her mad despair took now the form of a determination to commit suicide: so *spe concipere aliquid.*

477. **spem**] A Vergilian inversion for *spe frontem*. 'Shows the calm of hope upon her brow' instead of 'makes bright her brow with hope.'

482. **aptum**] here has its proper participial force. Generally it is an adj.

483. **Massylae**] seems to be used here generally for African. The Hesperides were daughters of Atlas to whom belonged the garden (called *templum* here in the sense probably of τέμενος a sacred enclosure) in which grew the golden apples, guarded by a dragon.

486. **papaver**] It would be such an unaccountable slip on Vergil's part to represent an opiate as the food of a sentinel-dragon, that it seems better to understand these words *spargens* &c. as connected with *servabat* only, and indicating some precaution against intruding animals, which might elude the dragon.

490. **videbis**] a not unusual confusion of terms expressing the action of the senses. Cf. Hor. Sat. II. viii. 77, *videres stridere secreta divisos aure susurros.*

493. **artes**] seems to be the only instance of an accus. after *accingor*. It is due here to the sense of *adhibere* implied. Cf. 137.

498. **iuvat**] The MSS. are divided between this and *iubet*. *Iubet monstratque* is rather a meaningless repetition. With *iuvat* the meaning is that what the priestess prescribes is in itself, apart from the relief promised, pleasurable to Dido.

502. **concipit**] 'realise.' *aut*=*nec*. Cf. 438.

504. **sub auras**] here and in 494, like *in auras* &c., means simply *high*.

506. **intendit**] from the meaning of 'stretches over,' with acc. and dat., Vergil deduces the sense-construction of acc. of the thing covered and abl. of the covering, as was regularly done in the case of *circumdo*, *obduco* and many of the verbs: so also *praetexere*, 500, 'to veil behind' instead of 'weave before.'

507. **super**] adv.

508. **haud ignara**] That is, she knew what was coming while the others did not. The words suggest very briefly the picture of Dido in calm despair preparing, unknown to those around her, her own funeral.

510. **ter centum**] like *sexcenti*, a vague large number.

Erebumque &c.] specimens of the gods invoked. *que* is appositional.

511. **Dianae**] Diana, corresponding to Greek Artemis, was in three forms, as the moon-goddess, the huntress, and Hecate a goddess of the lower world.

512. Avernus was a lake near Naples which was supposed to contain an entrance to the lower world. Its waters would be appropriate to a rite of this kind, but 'Vergil candidly admits that the Avernus water used on this occasion was not genuine.'

516. **amor**] 'The ancients believed that foals were born with tubercles on their foreheads, which were bitten off by their dams, and that if the tubercle was previously removed in

any other way (cf. *praereptus*) the dam refused to rear the foal. The name given to this flesh was *hippomanes*, and it was supposed to act as a love-charm (*amor*).' Con.

517. **mola manibusque**] qualify *testatur*, which includes the sense of *precatur*. 'With sprinkled meal and pious (upturned) hands makes her dying appeal to the gods.'

mola] sc. *salsa*, meal mixed with salt, used in sacrifices.

518. **pedem**] cf. 137. *exuta* is passive.

519. **moritura**] almost = *extremum*.

520. **non aequo**] 'one-sided love,' or 'ill-yoked lovers' (Con.): lit. 'those who love under the circumstances of a compact not evenly observed,' that is 'those whose lovers have proved false to their troth.'

521. **curae**] dat., *quod curae habet* = the more usual *cui curae est*.

526. **quae...lacus**] i.e. birds of the lakes or meres.

528. This line is generally regarded as an interpolation. If it is retained, there must be a pause in the construction at *ager*. Otherwise *tacent* is supplied to *pecudes &c.*

529. **at non**] *quievit* must be supplied from the sense of the previous lines.

animi] probably Graecising gen. cf. 203.

530. **solvitur**] 'cannot lull her strained nerves to slumber': cf. λυσιμελής 'limb-loosening,' an epithet of sleep in Homer.

noctem] 'the gift of night': *nox* = the effect of darkness to produce sightlessness, and inactivity of eyes and mind.

531. **rursus resurgens**] 're-rising again' = 'rising again and again.'

533. **insistit**] 'begins' to speak to herself. So with *ore* xii. 27. This is better than the other rendering 'perseveres.'

534. **inrisa**] proleptic, 'to be scorned by them.'

536. **totiens**] cf. 37, *ductoresque alii*.

537. **ultima iussa**] 'be at the beck and call,' Con. 'To perform the utmost commands' is 'to stop nowhere in obedience.'

538. **quiane**] '(why?) Because the aid I rendered them once stands me in good stead now?' That is, 'can I trust to

their gratitude for my past kindness to secure kind treatment from them?' It seems best to supply *me* to *iuvat* not *eos*, and render *iuvat* by 'helps' or 'boots,' as in Hor. Sat. I. i. 41 *Quid iuvat immensum te argenti pondus et auri Furtim defossa timidum deponere terra?* and Verg. Georg. II. 37.

540. **fac velle**] 'suppose I wished it,' a common use of *fac*, = 'put a case,' 'suppose.'

542. **Laomedonteae**] Laomedon was the Trojan king who defrauded the gods Apollo and Poseidon of the price for which they agreed to build the walls of Troy.

The epithet suggests that the descendants of such a king could be guilty of any fraud.

543—6. The sense of these lines is 'shall I follow Aeneas to Italy in a single ship, or take my whole people with me to find a new home as dependent allies of the Trojans?' The words *quos...revelli* forming part of the question practically supply the answer to it, by suggesting the impossibility of such a plan.

548—52. A mixture of self-reproach, reproach of her sister, and complaint against fate which would not let her preserve her loyalty to the memory of Sychaeus. 'And thou, my own sister, thou must be first to load me with these ills and cast me on the mercies of a foe! But thou could'st not bear my tears or see that I was mad. Oh! I could have lived like a thing of the woods, unwedded, unreproached, nor meddled with such cares. But it was not to be.' *more ferae* is a singularly unhappy expression, if it means, as it appears to mean, 'unfettered by the weaknesses of human nature.' If the literal meaning of 'beast-like' is to be pressed, *sine crimine* can only mean 'with no conscience to accuse me.'

553. **rumpebat**] for this use 'to let burst forth' cf. III. 246, *rumpitque hanc pectore vocem.*

554. **eundi**] obj. gen. after *certus*, but the usage is confined to poets, and post-Augustan prose.

556. **forma**] This is not a manifest unmistakeable appearance of Mercury as before, but '*a* divine shape *seen in a dream*, wearing the same look as before, *all like* to Mercury... which *seemed* to speak in the same warning accents.' In 577 Aeneas addressing this divine being says *quisquis es*, as if not certain who he was.

558. **omnia**] the so-called acc. of respect, really an imitation of the Greek use, e.g. *βοὴν ἀγαθός*.

coloremque] the *que* is elided before the *et* in the next line.

560. **sub casu**] 'at such a crisis.' *sub* has partly the sense of time, as in *sub nocte silenti*, and partly that of circumstance under which something happens.

561. **deinde**] 'in the near future,' or perhaps 'after what has happened.'

564. **mori**] This use of the infin. after adjs. is a Graecism of the Augustan poets.

565. **fugis**] 'art not flying?,' implying what M. had a right to expect to find him doing, is a more forcible way of saying, 'why art thou not flying?'

566. **iam**] anticipates *si...morantem*. If he stayed till morning, *by then* he would see &c.

trabibus] seems best understood of Dido's ships, and *turbari* of the effect of oars on the sea. The idea of the passage appears to be that the Carthaginian ships would surround the Trojans and set them on fire with materials previously prepared on land.

569. **varium**] cf. *triste lupus stabulis*. The effect of this construction is to give force to the attribute by representing the subject as a mass or piece of changeableness &c., so 'wholly changeable &c.,' 'a woman is all variableness and change.'

571. **umbris**] the apparition.

572. **corripit &c.**] 'awakes with a sudden start,' lit. 'hurriedly pulls his body together out of sleep.'

fatigare is 'to give no rest to.' So in entreaties, 'to wear out with prayers.' Here the idea seems to be that Aen. gave his followers no peace till he saw his orders carried out, 'in tones importunate calls on his men.'

573. **praecipites**] though coupled to *vigilate* is practically an independent exclamation. 'Head foremost my men!'='haste! haste! bestir yourselves! to your seats on the benches!'

577. **iterum**] grammatically connected with *paremus*, in sense rather qualifies *imperio*.

578. **sidera**] as influencing the weather, as Con. says; so that *sid. dextra* in prose = 'fair weather.'

caelo] locative abl.

581. **rapiuntque ruuntque**] The first verb is trans., the second intrans.; but both imply haste rather than any definite action, 'haste hands and feet.'

582. **deseruere**] pf. of instantaneous action; cf. Georg. I. 330 *Terra tremit; fugere ferae.*

587. **aequatis**] 'with levelled line of sails.' The ships advanced all together.

589. **percussa...abscissa**] middle, cf. 137.

591. **inluserit**] indignant use of perf. fut. The idea of the use seems to be 'shall so and so be allowed to become an accomplished fact?' Cf. IX. 784, *unus homo...tantas strages impune per urbem ediderit?*

593. **alii**] corresponds to an *alii* implied in what has gone before.

595. **mentem**] her 'purpose' as expressed 547.

596. **facta impia**] Aeneas' in the first sentence, her own in the second. 'Dost only now feel the sting of unholy deeds (that is, Aeneas' desertion)? Thou shouldst have felt it then when &c.' If she had felt her own unnatural behaviour towards Sychaeus more keenly, she would not have to mourn over Aeneas' ill-treatment of her.

599. **quem**] sc. *eius.*

603. The sense of the passage is, 'But it may be said (*verum = at enim*) the issue of such a battle might have been uncertain. Suppose it had been: what then? I am going to die in any case. If I had died in battle I could have killed my hated guest first.'

fuerat] vivid indic. for subj. 'it had been' = 'it would have been.' *fuisset*, 'let it have been' = 'grant that it would have been.'

604. **tulissem**] cond. (If I had done as I say) I should, might have &c. *exstinxem = exstinxissem.* So *surrexe = surrexisse* (Horace).

607. **lustras**] cf. 6. With this address compare Soph. Aj. 845.

609. **Hecate**] 511.

Dirae] the Furies 473. The Eumenides and Erinyes of the Greeks. They carried out the sentence of the gods on human offenders in certain cases.

610. **di**] a very obscure phrase; the gods of the lower world are meant to whom she consigns herself by death.

611. **meritum**] pass., deserved, well-earned.

614. **haeret**] depends on *si*.

615. All these things did happen to Aeneas: he was opposed by bitter enemies the Rutulians; he had to leave Ascanius in the camp while he went to seek aid from Evander; the final peace involved concessions to the Latins; and his body did not receive burial, being drowned in the Numicius. But they happened in such a way as to add to his ultimate glory, and to make the Romans proud of their ancestor, as the feud between Carthage and Rome also furnished proud memories to the Romans.

620. **inhumatus**] Dido prays that Aen. may suffer the premature death he is bringing on her and, worse than that, may suffer the evils after death which awaited those who lacked burial.

623. **cineri**] cf. Hor. Odes, II. i. 28 *rettulit inferias Iugurthae*.

625. **aliquis**] 'Arise O some one from my bones to avenge me, to chase &c.' Comp. Tennyson, In Memoriam, 'O somewhere meek unconscious dove &c.'

627. **nunc, olim**] 'now, or hereafter, whenever strength is given to do it.' For the asyndetism comp. *serius, ocius* &c.

629. **inprecor &c.**] 'Be shore opposed to shore &c....that is my curse upon them.' Lit. 'I imprecate shores opposed to shores &c.' The substantives with their predicative qualifications form the objs. to *inprecor*.

nepotesque] cf. 558. This hypermetrical syllable when it occurs is almost always *que*.

ipsi] is the present generation of Tyrians and Trojans, *nepotes* their descendants. Some MSS. omit the *que* after *nepotes*. If that is the true reading, *inprecor* will be parenthetical, and *pugnent* the verb to all the subjects *litora* &c.; *ipsi* will = the men as opp. to the inanimate subjects mentioned before.

633. **suam**] Dido's. The reflexive is used because Dido is the virtual subj. of the passage.

635. **spargere**] bathing was a necessary preliminary in approaching the gods. *dic properet = dic ut properet.*

636. **monstrata**] that is, by the priestess.

637. **sic**] under these circumstances, i.e. when she has done all this.

640. **Dardanii rogum capitis**] go together; *flammae* is the dat. after *permittere*. 'The pyre of the Dardan life' is the pyre on which the image of Aen. was placed (508). With the gen. comp. πυραὶ νεκύων, Hom. Il. I. 52. Servius remarks on this 'she calls her own pyre his to avoid suspicion.' *curis* is 'love-cares' as in 1.

644. **genas**] 137. *interfusa* is passive.

645. The pyre was in the *atrium* under the *impluvium*, 494. Dido had been in her tower, 586.

647. **munus**] generally explained a gift sought not for this purpose, as though D. had asked for and obtained Aeneas' sword as a present. And so Ovid and Silius Italicus appear to have understood it. But, apart from the improbability of Dido's asking for such a present, it is certainly implied in 495 and 507 that this sword was accidentally left behind by Aen. The usual interpretation takes *non* closely with *hos*, *non in hos* equalling *in alios*. But it is quite possible, as Kv. points out, to take the *non* with the whole expression and explain, 'a gift not sought for this purpose, but an accidental gift as it were, which could be appropriately used for her suicide.' It is generally assumed that the sword mentioned in 261 was Dido's present; but, if *munera* includes the sword, Dido must have made it!

649. **lacrimis**] see Introduction.

651. **dum &c.**] qualifying *dulces*.

653. **vixi**] 'I have lived my life.' Cf. *vixerunt* 'they are dead.'

656. **recepi**] = sumpsi, re- giving the notion of what is due, as in *reddo*.

659. **os**] 137. *inpressa*, middle.

660. **sic, sic**] 'Servius is probably right in saying that as she says *sic*, *sic*, she stabs herself twice.' (Con.)

661. **hunc**] 'the fire that this my death will cause to be lighted,' 'the fire that follows this.'

662. **omina**] the sight of a death-pyre to a man setting out to found a new kingdom would be most discouraging according to ancient ideas. Servius says that funeral fires seen at sea betokened a storm.

663. **ferro**] 'sink helpless on the sword,' which would slip from her hand as she stabbed herself the second time.

667. **femineo**] cf. 235.

669. 'There is a significance in the words "if Carthage should one day fall" in the mouth of a Roman.' (Con.)

675. **hoc**] 'was this what it meant?' lit. was that (about which you spoke to me) this (which you are doing now)? So *τοῦτ' ἐκεῖνο*.

677. **primum**] cf. 371 *quae quibus anteferam?*

678. **vocasses**] 'thou would'st &c.' (if thou hadst dealt fairly with me) = *vocare debuisti*.

681. **crudelis**] Anna very naturally reproaches herself with cruelty for having unwittingly helped to bring about this cruel end. These lines may be rendered 'Did I rear &c.... only to be away &c.?' or placing a colon at *deos*, we may take *ut abessem?* as an indignant exclamation like, *te ut ulla res frangat!* 'I reared &c.: O to think that I should have been away &c.!'

685. **evaserat**] the tense expresses rapidity, as the perf. in 582. The accus. after *evado* is a *constructio ad sensum*, *evado* getting the notion of 'clearing' or 'surmounting,' and taking its case accordingly.

689. **stridit**] of the gurgling sound of the spouting blood.

693. Dying persons were regarded as victims consecrated to the gods below, and a lock of the hair cut off, just as the forelock of animal victims was cut off in consecration. Here the

meaning seems to be that Proserpina, not having had due notice of Dido's coming death, because it was *ante diem*, not natural (*fato*), nor a violent death brought about by some action of her own (*merita mors*), either would not or could not attend to the case, and therefore Iris is despatched to perform the ceremony of consecration without which the death could not be completed.

694. **obitus**] 'struggles to die.'

27

VOCABULARY.

a, ab, *from*

ăbeo, ire, ivi *and* ii, ĭtum, intr. *depart*

ablŭo, luĕre, lui, lūtum, tr. *wash off*

abnŭo, nuĕre, nui, tr. *nod dissent to*, *refuse*

ăbŏleo, ēre, ēvi, ĭtum, tr. *efface*, *destroy*

abrĭpio, ripĕre, ripui, reptum, tr. *tear away*, *seize by force*

abrumpo, rumpĕre, rūpi, ruptum, tr. *break short off*

abscindo, scindĕre, scĭdi, scissum, tr. *cleave away*, *tear*

abscondo, dĕre, dĭdi *and* di, dĭtum, tr. *conceal*

absum, esse, fui, intr. *be away*

absŭmo, sumĕre, sumpsi, sumptum, tr. *destroy*

ac, short form of *atque*, only used before consonants

accendo, dĕre, di, sum, tr. *kindle*, *inflame*

accingo, cingĕre, cinxi, cinctum, tr. *gird on*, *arm*; in pass. by sense constrn., *employ as weapon*, with accus. 493

accĭpio, cipĕre, cēpi, ceptum, tr. *receive*, *listen to*

ăcer, cris, cre, *keen*, *mettlesome*

ăcervus, i, m. *heap*

ăcies, ei, f. *line*, *line of sight*, *eye*

ad, *to*

ădeo, ire, ivi *and* ii, ĭtum, tr. *approach*

ădeo, adv. *to such an extent*, as enclitic emphasises the word it follows, *mark me!*

adfātus, ūs, m. *address*

adfor, fari, fatus, tr. dep. *address*

adgnosco, gnoscĕre, gnōvi, gnĭtum, tr. *recognise*

adgrĕdior, gredi, gressus, tr. dep. *attack*, *assail*, *accost*

adhuc, *still*

adĭgo, igĕre, ēgi, actum, tr. *drive*, *hurl*

adĭmo, imĕre, ēmi, emptum, tr. *take away*

adĭtus, ūs, m. *approach*

adlŏquor, loqui, locūtus, tr. dep. *address*

admŏneo, ēre, ui, ĭtum, tr. *warn*

admŏveo, movēre, mōvi, mōtum, tr. *move to*

adnĭtor, niti, nixus, intr. dep. *lean upon*, *use effort*

adno, are, intr. *swim to*

adnŭo, nuĕre, nui, nūtum, intr. *nod assent*

adquīro, quirĕre, quīsivi, quīsitum, tr. *gain*
adsīduus, a, um, *unceasing*
adsto, stare, stĭti, intr. *stand by*
adsum, esse, fui, intr. *be at hand, here*
adsurgo, surgĕre, surrexi, surrectum, intr. *rise towards, up*
advĕna, ae, c. *stranger*
adversor, ari, &c. intr. dep. *be opposed*
adversus, a, um, *opposite*
adverto, tĕre, ti, sum, tr. *turn to, attend* (turn the mind to)
aeger, gra, grum, *sick*
ăēnus, a, um, *of bronze*
aequo, are, &c. tr. *make equal*
aequor, ŏris, n. *ocean, water*
aequus, a, um, *equal, favorable*
aestus, ūs, m. *tide*
aetas, tātis, f. *age*
aeternus, a, um, *eternal*
aether, ĕris, m. *upper air, sky*, acc. aethera
aethĕrius, a, um, *belonging to the aether*, or *sky*
Aethīops, ŏpis, m. *Ethiopian*
Agamemnŏnius, a, um, *of Agamemnon*
ăger, gri, m. *field, land*
aggĕro, are, &c. tr. *pile, heap one on another*; iras, *wrath on wrath*
ăgīto, are, &c. tr. *stir, hunt*
agmen, ĭnis, n. *troop, marching line*
ăgo, agĕre, ēgi, actum, tr. *work, form, do*; se agere, agi, *move*; absol. 71, *hunt*
aio, ăis, ăit, aiunt, defect. *say*
āla, ae, f. *feather, wing*, 121 *troop*, see n.
ālātus, a, um, *winged*
albesco, bescĕre, intr. *grow white*
ălĭēnus, a, um, *belonging to another, strange*
ălĭquis *or* aliqui, aliqua, aliquod, adj. *some*
aliquis, aliquid, pron. *some one*
ălĭter, *otherwise*
alius, a, ud, *other, some*
ălo, alĕre, alui, altum *or* alitum, tr. *rear, cherish, nurse*
Alpīnus, a, um, *of the Alps*
altāria, ium, n. pl. *altar*
alter, a, um, *one* or *other* of two
alterno, are, tr. *do by turns*; in V. only in pres. part. and intr. *alternate, waver*
altum, i, n. *deep sea*
altus, a, um, *high*
ămārus, a, um, *bitter*
ambio, ire, ivi *and* ii, ĭtum, tr. *come round, conciliate*
ambo, ae, o, *both*
āmens, tis, adj. *distracted, mad*
āmitto, mittĕre, mīsi, missum, *tr. lose*
amnis, is, m. *river*
ămor, ōris, m. *love*
amplector, plecti, plexus, tr. dep. *embrace*
amplus, a, um, *large, grand*
an, *or?* introduces second of two questions. The first is sometimes not expressed but implied
anceps, cĭpĭtis, adj. *double-headed, -faced, doubtful*
angustus, a, um, *narrow*

ănīlis, e, *of an old woman*
ănĭma, ae, f. *breath, life, soul*
ănĭmus, i, m. *mind, heart*, pl. *spirit, courage*
annōsus, a, um, *full of years*
ante, prep. and adv. *before*, ante...quam, *before* (conj.)
antefĕro, ferre, tŭli, lātum, *tr. set before*
antīquus, a, um, *ancient, old*
ăper, pri, m. *boar*
ăpex, ĭcis, m. *crest, head*
Apollo, ĭnis, m. *Apollo*
apto, are, &c. tr. *get ready, equip*
aptus, a, um, *fitted, studded*
ăpud, *by, among, in the mind of*
ăqua, ae, f. *water*
ăquĭlo, ōnis, m. *north-wind, storm-wind*
ăquōsus, a, um, *watery, rainy*
āra, ae, f. *altar*
arbŏs, ŏris, f. *tree*
arcānus, a, um, *secret*
ardeo, dēre, si, sum, intr. *blaze, burn* (with desire)
ardor, ōris, m. *heat, ardour*
arduus, a, um, *steep, lofty, towering*
ărēna, ae, f. *sand*
ărēnōsus, a, um, *sandy*
arguo, guĕre, gui, gūtum, tr. *make clear, expose*
arma, orum, n. pl. *arms*
armo, are, &c. *tr. arm, equip*
armus, i, m. *shoulder*
ăro, are, &c. tr. *plough*
arrĭgo, rigĕre, rexi, rectum, tr. *erect, set up on end*
ārtus, ūs, m. *limb*
ărundo, ĭnis, f. *reed, shaft*
ărvum, i, n. *field*
arx, cis, f. *citadel, height, tower*
aspectus, ūs, m. *sight*
asper, era, erum, *rough*
aspĭcio, spicĕre, spexi, spectum, *tr. behold, see*
ast=**at**
astrum, i, n. *star*
at, *but, moreover, meanwhile*
āter, tra, trum, *black*
Atlas, ntis, m. *Atlas*, son of Iapetus and Clymene, who supported the sky on his shoulders, identified with Mt Atlas in W. Africa
atque, *and*, stronger form of que
ātrium, i, n. *hall, court*
attingo, tingĕre, tĭgi, tactum, tr. *reach*
attollo, tollĕre, tr. *rear, lift*
attŏno, are, ui, itum, tr. *astound*. In V. only used in perf. pass. part.
auctor, ōris, m. *originator, author*
audax, ācis, adj. *bold*
audeo, dēre, sus, intr. dep. *be bold, dare*
audio, ire, ivi *and* ii, ītum, tr. *hear*
aufĕro, auferre, abstŭli, ablātum, tr. *take away, carry off*
augur, ŭris, m. *one who interprets omens, augur, prophet*
aula, ae, f. *courtyard, hall*
Aulis, ĭdis, f. harbour in Boeotia where Agamemnon assembled the fleet against Troy
aura, ae, f. *breeze, air*
aurĕus, a, um, *golden*
auris, is, f. *ear*

Aurōra, ae, f. *Dawn-goddess*
aurum, i, n. *gold*
Ausŏnius, a, um, *Italian*. The Ausŏnes were a tribe in ancient times inhabiting Latium
auspex, ĭcis, m. *interpreter of bird-omens, guide*
auspicium, i, n. *auspice*
aut, *either, or*
autem, *but, however, moreover*
auxilium, i, n. *aid*
āvello, vellĕre, velli, volsum, tr. *tear away*
Āvernus, a, um, *belonging to lake Avernus* in Campania
āverto, tĕre, ti, sum, *tr. turn away, divert, avert; aversa tuetur, surveys with backward glance*
ăvis, is, f. *bird*
ăvus, i, m. *grandfather, ancestor*
axis, is, m. *axis*, round which the heavens revolved, *the heavens*

bacchor, ari, &c. intr. dep. *behave like bacchanal, rush wildly*
Bacchus, i, m. *Bacchus*, wine-God
barba, ae, f. *beard*
Barcaei, orum, m. *inhabitants of Barce*, town in the Cyrenaica
bellum, i, n. *war*
bĕnĕ, *well*
bĭdens, tis, f. *sheep*
bis, *twice*
bŏrĕas, ae, m. *north-wind, storm-wind*
brĕvĭter, *shortly, in few words*
būbo, ōnis, f. *owl*

cădo, cadĕre, cĕcĭdi, cāsum, intr. *fall*
caecus, a, um, *blind, hidden*
caedes, is, f. *bloodshed*
caelum, i, n. *sky*
caerŭlus, a, um, *deep blue, dark-coloured*, neut. pl. as subst.
callis, is, m. *path*
călor, ōris, m. *heat*
campus, i, m. *plain*
candeo, ēre, ui, intr. *be bright, white*
cănis, is, c. *dog*
căno, canĕre, cĕcĭni, cantum, tr. *sing, rehearse*
căpesso, pessĕre, pessivi, pessītum, tr. *seize, make for*
căpio, capĕre, cēpi, captum, *tr. take, hold, contain*
capra, ae, f. *she-goat*
căput, ĭtis, n. *head, life, soul*
carbăsus, i, f.; pl. carbasa, orum, n. *canvas*
căreo, ēre, ui, intr. *be without*
cărīna, ae, f. *keel, ship*
carmen, ĭnis, n. *song*
carpo, pĕre, psi, ptum, tr. *pull to pieces, crop, enjoy*
Carthāgo, ĭnis, f. *Carthage*
cārus, a, um, *dear*
castīgo, are, &c. tr. *chastise, keep in order*
castra, orum, n. pl. *camp*
cāsus, ūs, m. *falling, chance, conjuncture*
căterva, ae, f. *troop*
Caucăsus, i, m. mountain range between the Euxine and Caspian
causa, ae, f. *cause, pretext*

cautes, is, f. *rock*
cĕler, is, e, *swift*
cĕlĕro, are, &c. tr. *hasten*
celsus, a, um, *lofty*
centum, indecl. *hundred*
Cĕres, ĕris, f. *Ceres;* see legifer
cerno, cernĕre, crēvi, crētum, tr. *see*, *descry*
certămen, ĭnis, n. *strife*
certo, are, &c. intr. *vie*, *strive with all the might*
certus, a, um, *secure*, *determined*
cerva, ae, f. *doe*
cervus, i, m. *stag*
Chăŏs, n. a Power of the under-world, parent of Night and Erebus
chlămys, ȳdis, f. *scarf*, *mantle*
chŏrus, i, m. *dance*, *troop of dancers*
cieo, ciēre, cīvi, cĭtum, tr. *rouse*
cingo, gĕre, xi, ctum, tr. *gird*, *close in*
cĭnis, ĕris, m. *ash*, *embers*
circum, adv. and prep. *round*, *around*
circumdo, dăre, dĕdi, dătum, tr. *surround*, *gird*
Cĭthaeron, ōnis, m. mountain on borders of Attica and Boeotia
cĭtus, a, um, *quick*
clāmo, are, &c. tr. *call on*
clāmor, ōris, m. *shouting*
clārus, a, um, *bright*
classis, is, f. *fleet*
coepi, coepisse, defect. *begin*
coeptum, i, n. *purpose*
Coeus, i, m. Titan, son of Uranus and Gaea
cōgo, cogĕre, coēgi, coactum, tr. *muster*, *force*, *marshal*
cŏlo, colĕre, colui, cultum, tr. *cultivate*, *tend*, *pay honour to*, *worship*
cŏlōnus, i, m. *settler*
cŏlor, ōris, m. *colour*
cŏma, ae, f. *hair*
cŏmes, ĭtis, c. *companion*
cŏmĭtatus, ūs, m. *accompanying*, *retinue*, *train*
cŏmĭtor, ari, &c. tr. dep. *accompany*
commisceo, miscēre, miscui, mixtum, tr. *mingle*
commŏveo, movēre, mōvi, mōtum, tr. *stir*, *shake*
commūnis, e, *shared*, *common*, *joint*
compello, are, &c. tr. *address*
complexus, ūs, m. *embrace*
compōno, ponĕre, pŏsui, pŏsitum, tr. *put together*, *settle*
concĭpio, cipĕre, cēpi, ceptum, tr. *conceive*, *shape*, *realise*
concĭto, are, &c. tr. *rouse*
concŭtio, cutĕre, cussi, cussum, tr. *shake violently*
condo, dĕre, dĭdi, dĭtum, tr. *hide*
conficio, ficĕre, fēci, fectum, tr. *perform*, *complete*, *finish*, *wear out*
confio, pass. of conficio
cōnĭcio, icĕre, iēci, iectum, tr. *hurl*, *shoot home*
coniŭgium, i, n. *wedlock*
coniunx, iŭgis, c. *spouse*
conlābor, labi, lapsus, intr. dep. *fall together*, *faint*, *sink helpless*
conlūceo, ēre, intr. *shine together*, *in numbers*
cōnor, ari, &c. tr. and intr. dep. *endeavour*

conscendo, scendĕre, scendi, scensum, tr. *mount*
conscĭus, a, um, *conscious, privy to a secret*
consīdo, sidĕre, sēdi, sessum, intr. *settle, take seat*
consĭlium, i, n. *counsel, purpose*
consisto, sistĕre, stĭti, stĭtum, intr. *halt, make stand*
conspĭcio, spicĕre, spexi, spectum, tr. *behold*
consterno, sternĕre, strāvi, strātum, tr. *bestrew*
consŭlo, sulĕre, sului, sultum, tr. *consult*
contendo, tendĕre, tendi, tentum, intr. *contend, strive*
contĭnuo, *forthwith*
contrā, prep. and adv. *against, in reply*
contrārius, a, um, *opposite, opposed to*
cōnŭbium, i, n. *marriage*
convecto, are, tr. *convey hurriedly*
convĕnio, venire, vĕni, ventum, intr. *assemble*
convexus, a, um, *hollow, convex*, neut. pl. *dome*
convīvium, i, n. *banquet*
cor, cordis, n. *heart, mind*
cornu, ūs, n. *horn*
cŏrōna, ae, f. *chaplet*
cŏrōno, are, &c. tr. *crown*
corpus, ŏris, n. *body*
corrĭpio, ripĕre, ripui, reptum, tr. *raise hastily, catch*
crastĭnus, a, um, *of tomorrow*
crēdo, dĕre, dĭdi, dĭtum, intr. and tr. *believe, confide*
Crēs, Crētis, m. *a Cretan*
cresco, crescĕre, crēvi, crētum, intr. *grow*

Crēsius, a, um, *of Crete*
crīmen, ĭnis, n. *accusation, blame*
crīnis, is, m. *hair*
crŏcĕus, a, um, *saffron-coloured*
crūdēlis, e, *cruel*
crŭor, ōris, m. *blood* (spilt), *gore*
cŭbīle, is, n. *bed*
cŭbĭtus, i, m. *elbow, arm*
culmen, ĭnis, n. *top*
culpa, ae, f. *fault*
cum, prep. *with*, conj. *when*
cŭmŭlo, are, &c. tr. *heap*
cunctor, ari, &c. intr. *linger, hesitate*
cunctus, a, um, *all*
cŭpīdo, ĭnis, f. *lust, desire*
cŭpio, cupĕre, cupīvi, cupītum, tr. *desire*
cūr, *why*
cūra, ae, f. *care, love;* curae esse, *be for care, be under the charge;* curae habere, *have for care, care for*
cūro, are, &c. tr. *care for*
cursus, ūs, m. *course, running*
custōs, ōdis, c. *guardian*
Cyllenius, a, um, *of Cyllene*, Mt in Arcadia, epithet of Mercury born there
Cynthus, i, m. Mt in Delos, birthplace of Apollo
Cȳthērēa, ae, f. *Venus*, so called from the island of Cythera on the coast of which she first landed when she arose out of the foam of the sea

damno, are, &c. tr. *condemn*
Dănăi, um, m. *Greeks*
Dardănius, a, um, *Dardanian, Trojan*

Dardănus, i, m. founder and king of Troy
de, *from, about, according to*
dĕa, ae, f. *goddess*
dĕbeo, ēre, &c. tr. *owe*
dĕcēdo, cedĕre, cessi, cessum, intr. *withdraw*
dĕceo, ēre, ui, tr. *become, befit*, decet, impers.
dĕcĭpio, cipĕre, cēpi, ceptum, tr. *deceive*
dĕclīno, are, &c. tr. *droop*
dĕcōrus, a, um, *comely*
dĕcurro, currĕre, curri, cursum, intr. *run down*
dĕcus, ŏris, n. *grace, beauty, ornament*
dēdignor, ari, &c. tr. dep. *disdain*
dēdūco, ducĕre, duxi, ductum, tr. *lead down*
dĕfendo, fendĕre, fendi, fensum, tr. *defend*
dēfĕro, ferre, tŭli, lātum, tr. *carry down, report*
dēfĭcio, ficĕre, fēci, fectum, intr. *fail*
dĕgĕner, gĕnĕris, adj. *degenerate*
dēgo, degĕre, dēgi, tr. *spend, pass*
dĕhisco, hiscĕre, intr. *yawn, gape, open*
dēĭcio, icĕre, iēci, iectum, tr. *throw down, dislodge*
deinde (dissyl.), *next*
dēlĭgo, ligĕre, lēgi, lectum, tr. *choose*
Dēlos, i, f. *Delos*, one of the Cyclades islands where Apollo was born
dēlūbrum, i, n. *shrine*
dēmens, tis, adj. *infatuated, mad*
dēmitto, mittĕre, mīsi, missum, tr. *send, let down, admit*
dērĭpio, ripĕre, ripui, reptum, tr. *tear down*
desaevio, vire, vii, vītum, intr. *spend one's wrath*
descendo, scendere, scendi, scensum, intr. *descend*
dēsĕco, secare, secui, sectum, tr. *cut off*
dēsĕro, serĕre, serui, sertum, tr. *abandon*
dēsĭno, sinĕre, sii, situm, intr. *cease*
despĭcio, spicĕre, spexi, spectum, tr. *look down on, slight*
destrŭo, struĕre, struxi, structum, tr. *pull down, destroy*
dēsŭper, *from above*
dētĭneo, tinēre, tinui, tentum, tr. *hold back, detain*
dētorqueo, torquēre, torsi, tortum, tr. *turn away, bend*
dĕus, i, m. *god*
dēvĕnio, venire, vēni, ventum, tr. *come down to, reach*
dēvŏlo, are, &c. intr. *fly down*
dexter, ĕra *and* ra, erum *and* rum, *right-handed, propitious*
dextĕra *and* dextra, ae, f. *right-hand*
Dīāna, ae, f. *Diana*, sister of Apollo
dīco, dicĕre, dixi, dictum, tr. *say*
dĭco, are, &c. tr. *dedicate, assign*
Dictaeus, a, um, *Cretan*, from Dicte, Mt in Crete
dictum, i, n. *word*

Dīdo, ūs, f. *Dido*, Carthaginian queen
dĭēs, ei, m. & f. *day*
diffĭcilis, e, *difficult, hard*
diffŭgio, fugĕre, fūgi, intr. *fly in different directions*
diffundo, fundĕre, fūdi, fūsum, tr. *scatter, sow broadcast*
dignor, ari, &c. tr. dep. *deem worthy*
dignus, a, um, *worthy*
dīgrĕdior, gredi, gressus, intr. dep. *part, disperse*
dīlābor, labi, lapsus, intr. dep. *glide away, depart*
dīlĭgo, ligĕre, lexi, lectum, tr. *love*
dīmoveo, movĕre, mōvi, mōtum, tr. *divide, dislodge*
Dīra, ae, f. *fury*
dīrus, a, um, *dreadful*
Dīs, ītis, *Pluto*, as Zeus (Dis) of the lower world
discerno, cernĕre, crēvi, crētum, tr. *distinguish, pick out*
dissĭmŭlo, are, &c. tr. *dissimulate, conceal*
dīvello, vellĕre, velli, volsum, tr. *tear asunder*
dīversus, a, um, *in different directions*
dīves, ĭtis, adj. *rich*
dīvĭdo, vidĕre, vīsi, visum, tr. *divide*
dīvus, a, um, *divine*, as subst. *god, goddess*, gen. pl. divom
do, dăre, dĕdi, dătum, tr. *give, allow*
dŏceo, docĕre, docui, doctum, tr. *teach*
dŏleo, ēre, ui, intr. *grieve, be indignant*
dŏlor, ōris, m. *pain, indignation*
dŏlus, i, m. *deceit, stratagem*
dŏmĭnus, i, m. *owner, lord*
dŏmus, ūs, f. *house, home*
dōnum, i, n. *gift*
dōtālis, e, *belonging to a dower*
drăco, ōnis, m. *serpent, dragon*
Drȳŏpes, um, m. Pelasgian tribe originally settled in the neighbourhood of Parnassus
dŭbius, a, um, *doubtful, wavering*
dūco, ducĕre, duxi, ductum, tr. *lead, draw, prolong*
ductor, ōris, m. *leader*
dulcis, e, *sweet, dear*
dum, *while*
dūmus, i, m. *thorn*
dŭo, ae, o, *two*
dŭplex, ĭcis, adj. *double, two*
dūrus, a, um, *hard*
dux, dŭcis, m. *leader*

e, **ex**, *from, out of*
ecce, *behold!*
ĕdo, edĕre, ēdi, ēsum, tr. *eat*
effĕro, efferre, extŭli, ēlātum, tr. *bring forth, lift*
effĕrus, a, um, *wild, maddened*
effĭgies, ei, f. *image, statue*
effor, fari, &c. tr. dep. *speak out*
effundo, fundĕre, fūdi, fūsum, tr. *pour out, let stream*
ĕgeo, ēre, ui, intr. *be in need*
ĕgo, mĕi, first pers. pron.
ēgrĕgius, a, um, *noble*
ēĭcio, eicĕre, eiēci, eiectum, tr. *cast out*
Ĕlissa, ae, f. another name of Dido
ēn, *see!*

Encĕlădus, i, m. giant, son of Uranus and Gaea
ĕnim, *for, indeed*
ēnĭteo, ēre, ui, intr. *shine out*
ensis, is, m. *sword*
ēnŭmĕro, are, &c. tr. *recount*
ĕo, ire, ivi and ii, ĭtum, intr. *go*
ĕpŭlae, arum, f. pl. *feast*
ĕpŭlor, ari, &c. intr. dep. *feast*, *tr.* 602
ĕques, ĭtis, m. *horseman*
ĕquĭdem, *for my own part*, strengthened form of quidem, but always used with first pers. in Class. Latin
ĕquus, i, m. *horse*
Ĕrĕbus, i, m. *the underworld*
ergo, *therefore*
ērĭgo, rigĕre, rexi, rectum, tr. *erect, rear*
ērĭpio, ripĕre, ripui, reptum, *tr. seize, snatch*
erro, are, &c. intr. *wander*
ērŭo, uĕre, ui, ŭtum, tr. *root up*
et, *and, both, also*
ĕtiam, *also*
Eumenides, um, f. *Eumenides, Furies* = Dirae
ēvānesco, nescĕre, nui, intr. *vanish, melt away*
ēvinco, vincĕre, vīci, victum, *tr. overpower*
ēvŏco, are, &c. tr. *call forth, summon*
exănĭmis, e, *lifeless, fainting, with sinking heart*
exaudio, ire, ivi, itum, tr. *hear from out* of something
excieo, ciēre, civi *and* cii, citum, tr. *rouse*
excĭpio, cipĕre, cēpi, ceptum, tr. *receive, take up, answer, catch*
excŭbiae, arum, f. pl. *watchkeeping, watch-fires, sentries*
exerceo, cēre, cui, citum, *tr. work, press forward, harass*
exhaurio, haurire, hausi, haustum, tr. *draw off, bear to the end*
exigo, igĕre, ēgi, actum, tr. *work out, plan*
exĭguus, a, um, *small, scanty*
exordium, i, n. *beginning*
exŏrior, oriri, ortus, intr. dep. *arise*
expĕdio, ire, ivi and ii, itum, *tr. disentangle, get ready*
expĕrior, periri, pertus, tr. dep. *try*
expers, tis, adj. *without share, ignorant of*
exposco, poscĕre, poposci, tr. *entreat*
exquīro, quirĕre, quīsivi, quīsitum, *tr. seek for earnestly*
exscindo, scindĕre, scĭdi, scissum, tr. *destroy, root out*
exsĕquor, sequi, secūtus, tr. dep. *follow out, perform*
exsolvo, solvĕre, solvi, solūtum, tr. *release*
exspecto, are, &c. tr. *await, tarry*
exstinguo, stinguĕre, stinxi, stinctum, tr. *blot out*
exstruo, struĕre, struxi, structum, tr. *build up, rear*
exta, orum, n. pl. *entrails*
extemplo, *forthwith*
exterreo, terrēre, terrui, territum, *tr. terrify*
extĕrus, a, um, *outside, foreign*
extorris, e, *exiled*

extremus, a, um, *last, furthest*, superl. of exterus
exŭo, uĕre, ui, ūtum, tr. *uncover, bare, discard*
exŭviae, arum, f. pl. *relics*

facesso, cessĕre, cessi, cessītum, tr. *take in hand eagerly, fulfil*
facilis, e, *easy*
făcio, facĕre, fēci, factum, tr. *do;* fac, *suppose*
factum, i, n. *deed*
fallo, fallĕre, fefelli, falsum, tr. *deceive*
falx, cis, f. *sickle, knife*
fāma, ae, f. *report;* personified, *Rumour*
fămŭla, ae, f. *handmaid*
fămŭlus, i, m. *manservant*
far, farris, n. *spelt*
fas, indecl. *that which is allowed by law of gods, privilege*
fātālis, e, *fated, given by fates*
făteor, ēri, fassus, tr. dep. *confess*
fătīgo, are, &c. tr. *worry, give no rest to, rouse*
fātum, i, n. *fate*
faux, cis, f. *jaw*, pl. *throat*
fax, făcis, f. *torch*
fēlix, īcis, adj. *fortunate*
fēmĭna, ae, f. *woman*
fēmĭneus, a, um, *of a woman*
fĕra, ae, f. *wild beast, game*
fērālis, e, *of death*
fĕrio, ire, tr. *strike*
fĕro, ferre, tŭli, lātum, tr. *bear, report;* pass. *move, grope*
fĕrox, ōcis, adj. *high-spirited, mettlesome*
ferrum, i, n. *steel*
fertĭlis, e, *fertile*
fĕrus, a, um, *savage, wild*
ferveo, vēre *and* vĕre, vui *and* bui, intr. *be hot, busy*
fessus, a, um, *weary*
festīno, are, &c. tr. *hasten*
festus, a, um, *festive*
fībula, ae, f. *brooch, pin*
fictum, i, n. *falsehood*
fĭdes, ei, f. *faith, belief*
fīgo, gĕre, xi, xum, tr. *fix, pierce*
fingo, fingĕre, finxi, fictum, tr. *shape, invent, imagine*
fīnis, is, m. *end, border*
flāmen, ĭnis, n. *blast*
flamma, ae, f. *flame*
flātus, ūs, m. *breath, blast*
flāveo, ēre, intr. *be yellow, golden*
flāvus, a, um, *yellow, golden*
flecto, flectĕre, flexi, flexum, tr. *bend*
flētus, ūs, m. *weeping*
flōreo, ēre, ui, intr. *bloom, flourish*
flos, ōris, m. *flower*
fluctuo, are, &c. intr. *wave, surge*
fluctus, ūs, m. *wave, billow*
flŭentum, i, n. *stream*
flūmen, ĭnis, n. *river*
flŭo, fluĕre, fluxi, fluxum, intr. *flow*
flŭvĭālis, e, *of a stream*
flŭvius, i, m. *stream*
foedo, are, &c. tr. *disfigure*
foedus, a, um, *foul, disfigured*
foedus, ĕris, n. *treaty*
fons, tis, m. *spring, water*
for, fari, &c. tr. dep. *speak, say*

forma, ae, f. *shape, figure*
formīca, ae, f. *ant*
forsan, *perhaps*
fortis, e, *brave, stalwart*
fortūna, ae, f. *fortune*
forus, i, m. *deck*
fŏveo, fovēre, fōvi, fōtum, tr. *keep warm, cherish, cling to, make most of*
frāter, tris, m. *brother*
frāternus, a, um, *of a brother*
fraudo, are, &c. tr. *rob*
fraus, dis, f. *deceit, guile*
frĕmo, ĕre, ui, itum, intr. *shout*
frēnum, i, n. *bridle*
frētus, a, um, *relying*
frīgidus, a, um, *cold*
frondeo, ēre, intr. *be leafy*
frons, dis, f. *leaf, foliage*
frons, tis, f. *forehead*
frūmentum, i, n. *corn*
frŭor, frui, intr. dep. *reap fruit, enjoy*
frustrā, *in vain*
fŭga, ae, f. *flight*
fŭgio, fugĕre, fūgi, tr. and intr. *fly from, fly*
fulcio, cire, si, tum, tr. *prop, support*
fulgeo, gēre, si, intr. *shine, glitter*
fulmen, ĭnis, n. *lightning*
fulmĭnĕus, a, um, *lightning-like, flashing*
fulvus, a, um, *tawny*
fundāmentum, i, n. *foundation*
fundo, are, &c. tr. *found*
fundo, fundĕre, fūdi, fūsum, tr. *pour, overthrow*
fūnĕrĕus, a, um, *belonging to death, funereal*
fūnis, is, m. *rope*
fūnus, eris, n. *funeral, death*
fŭria, ae, f. *fury, demon*
fŭrĭbundus, a, um, *wild, maddened*
fŭro, furĕre, furui, intr. *be wild, run madly*
fŭror, ōris, m. *madness, passion*
furtīvus, a, um, *stealthy*
furtum, i, n. *stealth*
fŭturum, i, n. *the future*

Gaetūlus, a, um, *Gaetulian*. The Gaetuli were an African people who lived south of the Mauri and Numidians
Gărămantis, idis, f. adj. *belonging to the Garamantes*, people of Libya
gaudeo, gaudēre, gāvīsus, intr. *rejoice*
gĕlu, ūs, n. *cold, frost*
gĕmĭnus, a, um, *double*
gĕmĭtus, ūs, m. *groaning*
gĕmo, gemĕre, gemui, gemitum, intr. *groan*
gĕna, ae, f. *cheek*
gĕnĭtor, ōris, m. *father*
gĕnĭtrix, trīcis, f. *mother*
gens, tis, f. *race*
gĕnus, ĕris, n. *race, stock, kind*
germānus, i, m. *brother*; germana, ae, f. *sister*
gigno, gignĕre, gĕnui, gĕnitum, tr. *beget*
glăcies, ei, f. *ice*
glădius, i, m. *sword*
glŏmĕro, are, &c. tr. *make into a ball, mass*
glōria, ae, f. *glory*
grădior, gradi, gressus, intr. dep. *walk*

grădus, ūs, m. *step*
Graius, a, um (gen. pl. Graium), *Greek*
grāmen, ĭnis, n. *grass*
grandis, e, *large*
grando, ĭnis, f. *hail*.
gratia, ae, f. *favor, gratitude*
grātor, ari, &c. intr. *wish joy*
grăvidus, a, um, *pregnant*
grăvis, e, *heavy*
grĕmium, i, n. *bosom*
Grȳnēus, a, um, *of Grynium*, town on coast of Aeolis, with a celebrated temple and oracle of Apollo

hăbeo, ēre, ui, itum, tr. *have, hold*
haereo, rēre, si, sum, intr. *stick, remain*
hālitus, ūs, m. *breath*
Hammon, ōnis, m. surname of the Libyan Jupiter
haud, *not*
haurio, rire, si, stum, tr. *draw, drink, drain the cup of*
Hecate, es, f. *Hecate*, a night-worshipped power of the underworld, identified with Diana as the moon-goddess
heia, interj. *Ho!*
herba, ae, f. *grass*
hēres, ēdis, m. *heir*
hēros, ōis, m. *hero*
Hespĕria, ae, f. *Italy*
Hespĕrides, um, f. pl. daughters of Atlas and Hesperia, who dwelt in a garden, guarded by a dragon, in which the golden apples grew
heu, interj. *alas!*
hībernus, a, um, *wintry*
hic, haec, hoc, *this* (near the speaker)
hīc, *here, hereupon*
hiemps, hiĕmis, f. *winter*
hinc, *hence;* hinc...hinc (illinc), *on this side...on that side*
hŏnos, ōris, m. *honor, glory*
hōra, ae, f. *hour*
horreo, ēre, ui, intr. and tr. *be rough, shudder at*
horridus, a, um, *rough, bristling, awful*
horrifico, are, &c. tr. *horrify*
hospes, ĭtis, c. *guest*
hospitium, i, n. *hospitality*
hostis, is, c. *foe*
hūc, *hither;* huc...illuc (atque huc), *this way and that*
hŭmilis, e, *low, lowly*
hȳmĕnaeus, i, m. *bridal-song, wedding*
Hyrcānus, a, um, *belonging to Hyrcania*, country bordering on the Caspian Sea

iacto, are, &c. tr. *toss*
iam, *now, by this time;* iam... iam, *at one time...at another time*
iamdūdum, *long since, this long while*
iaspis, ĭdis, f. *jasper*
īdem, ĕadem, ĭdem, *the same*
ideo, *therefore, for that*
igitur, *therefore, well then!*
ignārus, a, um, *ignorant*
ignĕus, a, um, *fiery*
ignis, is, m. *fire*
ignōtus, a, um, *unknown*
īlex, ĭcis, f. *holm-oak*
Iliăcus, a, um, *of Ilium, Trojan*
ille, a, ud, *that* (remote from the speaker), *he*

Imāgo, ĭnis, f. *likeness*
imber, bris, m. *rain*
immānis, e, *enormous, huge*
immisceo, miscēre, miscui, mixtum, tr. *mingle in*
immōtus, a, um, *unmoved, unshaken*
impĕrium, i, n. *command*
impius, a, um, *lost to sense of natural duty, godless, unnatural, monster*
impleo, plēre, plēvi, plētum, tr. *fill*
imprŏbus, a, um, *wicked*
īmus, a, um, *lowest*
in, with abl. *in*, with accus. *into*
ĭnānis, e, *empty, useless, leisure*
incautus, a, um, *unawares, off his (her) guard*
incēdo, cedĕre, cessi, cessum, intr. *walk erect*
incendo, cendĕre, cendi, censum, tr. *set on fire, kindle, torture*
inceptum, i, n. *undertaking, purpose*
incertus, a, um, *uncertain*
incīdo, cidĕre, cīdi, cisum, tr. *cut*
incĭpio, cipĕre, cēpi, ceptum, tr. *begin*
inclūdo, cludĕre, clusi, clusum, tr. *shut in*
incŏmĭtatus, a, um, *solitary*
incŭbo, cubare, cubui, cubitum, intr. *recline*
incumbo, cumbĕre, cubui, cubitum, intr. *rest on, lay weight on, lie down on*
indāgo, ĭnis, f. *encircling, circle of nets*
indignus, a, um, *unworthy*
indulgeo, gēre, si, tum, intr. *give play, indulge*
iners, tis, adj. *helpless*
inexpertus, a, um, *untried*
infăbrĭcatus, a, um, *unformed, rough*
infandus, a, um, *unspeakable, horrible*
infectus, a, um, *not-done, fictitious*
infēlix, īcis, adj. *unsuccessful, unhappy*
infensus, a, um, *hostile, angry*
infĕro, ferre, tŭli, lātum, tr. *carry*, pass. *advance*
infīgo, figĕre, fixi, fixum, tr. *fix in, on*
inflammo, are, &c. tr. *kindle, inflame*
inflecto, flectĕre, flexi, flexum, tr. *bend*
infrēnus, a, um, *unbridled*
infundo, fundĕre, fūdi, fūsum, tr. *pour on, in*
ingĕmino, are, &c. intr. *double*
ingĕmo, gemĕre, gemui, intr. *groan*
ingens, tis, adj. *huge*
ingrĕdior, gredi, gressus, intr. *march on, stalk*
inhio, are, &c. intr. *gape, pore*
inhospitus, a, um, *inhospitable*
inhŭmatus, a, um, *unburied*
inĭcio, icĕre, iēci, iectum, tr. *fling, cast on*
inĭmīcus, a, um, *hostile*
inīquus, a, um, *uneven*
iniūria, ae, f. *wrong*
inlūdo, dĕre, si, sum, intr. *make sport, mock*
inmĕmor, ŏris, adj. *forgetful, regardless*

inmitto, mittĕre, mīsi, missum, tr. *send into, let loose on*

innecto, nectĕre, nexui, nexum, *tr. weave together, string*

inops, ŏpis, adj. *powerless*

inpello, pellĕre, pŭli, pulsum, *tr. drive on, dash in*

inplĭco, are, ui, itum, tr. *twine, fasten up*

inplōro, are, &c. tr. *implore*

inpōno, ponĕre, posui, positum, tr. *set on*

inprĕcor, ari, &c. tr. dep. *pray for something against a person;* 'be shore at feud with shore, such is my prayer' 629

inprīmo, primĕre, pressi, pressum, tr. *impress*

inrīdeo, ridĕre, rīsi, risum, tr. *laugh at, mock*

inrīto, are, &c. tr. *vex, exasperate*

inrumpo, rumpĕre, rūpi, ruptum, tr. *burst into, through*

insania, ae, f. *madness*

insĕquor, qui, cutus, tr. dep. *follow on*

insignis, e, *conspicuous*

insisto, sistĕre, stĭti, intr. *set foot on, begin, persist*

insomnis, e, *sleepless*

insomnium, i, n. *dream*

instauro, are, &c. tr. *renew*

instĭmŭlo, are, &c. tr. *goad, spur on, urge*

insto, stare, stĭti, intr. *press on, be urgent, lie near*

insŭpĕrabilis, e, *invincible*

intendo, dĕre, di, sum, *and* tum, *stretch, stretch on, cover*

inter, *between, among*

intĕrĕa, *meanwhile*

interfundo, fundĕre, fūdi, fūsum, tr. *pour between*

intĕrior, ius, *inner*

interpres, ĕtis, c. *go-between, agent, medium*

interrumpo, rumpĕre, rūpi, ruptum, tr. *break off, interrupt*

intro, are, &c. tr. *enter*

intŭs, *within*

inultus, a, um, *unavenged*

invādo, dĕre, si, sum, *tr. attack, accost*

invĕnio, venire, vēni, ventum, tr. *find*

invĭdeo, vidēre, vīdi, vīsum, tr. *grudge*

invĭdia, ae, f. *grudge*

invīso, visĕre, vīsi, vīsum, tr. *visit*

invīsus, a, um, *hated*

invītus, a, um, *unwilling*

invīus, a, um, *pathless, impassable*

ipse, a, um, *self, very*

Ira, ae, f. *anger*

Iris, ĭdis, f. *Iris*, rainbow-messenger of gods

Is, ĕa, ĭd, *this, that*

iste, a, ud, *that* (with reference to second person)

Ita, *so*

Ĭtălus, a, um, *Italian.* Italia, *Italy*

Iter, itĭnĕris, n. *journey, way*

Itĕrum, *a second time*

iŭbar, ăris, n. *ray*

iŭbeo, iubĕre, iussi, iussum, tr. *command*

iŭgalis, e, *of wedlock*

iŭgum, i, n. *yoke, hill-ridge*

iungo, gĕre, xi, ctum, tr. *join*
Iūno, ōnis, f. *Juno*, wife of Jupiter
Iuppiter, Iŏvis, m. *Jupiter*
iūro, are, &c. intr. *swear*
ius, iūris, n. *right*
iussum, i, n. *command*
iustus, a, um, *just*
iŭventa, ae, f. *youth* (abstr.)
iŭventus, ūtis, f. *youth* (collect.)
iŭvo, iuvare, iūvi, iūtum, tr. *help, please*
iuxta, *near, close to*

lăbĕfăcio, facĕre, fēci, factum, tr. *make to totter, stagger*
lăbo, are, &c. intr. *waver*
lăbor, ōris, m. *toil*
lābor, bi, psus, intr. dep. *glide, move silently and quickly*
lacrĭma, ae, f. *tear*
lac, lactis, n. *milk*
lăcus, ūs, m. *lake*
laena, ae, f. *mantle*
laetus, a, um, *glad*
lāmentum, i, n. *lamentation*
lampas, adis, f. *torch, lamp*
Lāŏmĕdontēus, a, um, *of Laomedon*, founder of Troy, who cheated the gods
lātē, *widely, far and wide*
lăteo, ēre, ui, intr. *lie hid*
lătex, ĭcis, m. *water*
laus, dis, f. *honour*
Lăvīnius, a, um, *belonging to Lavinium*, city of Latinus
lectus, i, m. *couch*
lēgĭfer, era, erum, *law-bringing, founder of law*, epithet of Ceres, the introduction of settled law following on that of agriculture
lĕgo, legĕre, lēgi, lectum, tr. *choose*. lectus, adj. *choice*.
Lēnaeus, a, um, *of Bacchus*, as god of the wine-press (ληνός)
lēnio, ire, ivi, itum, tr. *soothe, negotiate*
lĕo, ōnis, m. *lion*
lētālis, e, *deadly*
lētum, i, n. *death*
lĕvo, are, &c. tr. *lighten*
lex, lēgis, f. *law*, pl. *conditions, terms*
lībo, are, &c. tr. *sip, pour in libation*
lībro, are, &c. tr. *poise*
Lĭbўa, ae, f. *Libya*
Lĭbўcus, a, um, *of Libya*
lĭcet, ēre, uit, impers. *it is lawful*
limbus, i. m. *stripe, border*
līmen, ĭnis, n. *doorway*
lingua, ae, f. *tongue*
linquo, linquĕre, līqui, lictum, tr. *leave, abandon*
līquĭdus, a, um, *liquid*
lĭto, are, &c. tr. *perform* (sacrifice) *with favorable omens*
lītus, ŏris, n. *coast*
lŏco, are, &c. tr. *place*
lŏcus, i, m. (pl. loca), *place, room*
longus, a, um, *long, tedious*
lŏquor, loqui, locutus, tr. dep. *speak*
luctor, ari, &c. intr. dep. *wrestle, struggle*
lūdus, i, m. *sport, game*
lūmen, ĭnis, n. *light, eye*
lūna, ae, f. *moon*
lustro, are, &c. tr. *survey, traverse*
lustrum, i, n. *lair*

lux, lūcis, f. *light*
luxus, ūs, m. *luxury*
Lȳaeus, i, m. *Bacchus*, as the looser (λύω) from cares
Lycia, ae, f. *Lycia*, territory of Asia Minor between Caria and Pamphylia

māchĭna, ae, f. *engine*
macto, are, &c. tr. *sacrifice*
măcŭla, ae, f. *spot*
mădeo, ēre, ui, intr. *be wet*
Maeŏnius, a, um, *Maeonian, Lydian, Asiatic*
maereo, ēre, ui, intr. *mourn*
māgālia, ium, n. pl. *huts, low buildings on outskirts of Carthage*
măgĭcus, a, um, *magic*
măgis, *more*
magnus, a, um, great, comp. major
mălĕ, *badly*, scarce
mālo, malle, malui, tr. *prefer*
mălum, i, n. *evil*
mandatum, i, n. *command*
mando, are, &c. tr. *commit, entrust, command*
mando, dĕre, di, sum, tr. *champ*
măneo, ēre, si, sum, tr. and intr. *remain, await*
Mānes, ium, m. pl. *souls of the departed, the invisible world*
mănĭca, ae, f. *sleeve*
mănifestus, a, um, *palpable, unmistakeable*
mănus, ūs, f. *hand, power, troop*
măre, is, n. *sea*
mărītus, i, m. *husband*
marmor, ŏris, n. *marble*
marmŏreus, a, um, *of marble*
Mars, tis, m. *Mars*, god of war
Martius, a, um, *of Mars, martial*
Massȳlus, a, um, *belonging to Massyli*, Numidian tribe
māternus, a, um, *maternal*
Maurūsius, a, um, *belonging to Mauretania, Moorish*
mĕdĭtor, ari, &c. tr. dep. *think of, plan*
mĕdius, a, um, *middle*
mĕdulla, ae, f. *marrow*
mel, mellis, n. *honey*
membrum, i, n. *limb*
mĕmini, meminisse, tr. and intr. def. *be mindful, remember*
mĕmor, ŏris, adj. *having memory, thoughtful*
mĕmŏrābilis, e, *worth recording, memorable*
mĕmŏro, are, &c. tr. *mention, speak of*
mens, tis, f. *mind, purpose*
mentum, i, n. *chin*
Mercŭrius, i, m. *Mercury*
mĕreo, ēre, ui, itum, *and* mĕreor, ēri, itus, tr. *deserve*
mĕrĭtum, i, n. *service*
mĕto, metĕre, messui, messum, tr. *reap*
mĕtuo, uĕre, ui, tr. *fear*
mĕus, a, um, *my*
mīgro, are, &c. intr. *move, shift abode*
mīna, ae, f. *threat*
mīrābilis, e, *wondrous*
mīrus, a, um, *wonderful*
misceo, miscēre, miscui, mixtum, and mistum, tr. *mingle, confound*
miser, era, erum, *wretched*

mĭsĕrābĭlis, e, *pitiable, piteous*
mĭsĕreor, ēri, intr. dep. *feel pity*, obj. in gen.
miseror, ari, &c. tr. *pity*
mĭtra, ae, f. *cap, turban*
mitto, mittĕre, mīsi, missum, tr. *send*
mōbĭlĭtas, tis, f. *supple movement*
mŏdŏ, *only*
mŏdus, i, m. *manner, limit*
moenia, ium, n. pl. *walls*
mŏla, ae, f. *meal;* mola salsa, mixture of bruised grain and salt used in sacrifices
mōlior, iri, itus, dep. *labour at, use effort to do, task oneself to do*
mollis, e, *soft, yielding*
mŏneo, ēre, ui, itum, tr. *advise*
mŏnĭmentum, i, n. *record*
mŏnĭtum, i, n. *warning words*
monitus, ūs, m. *warning*
mons, tis, m. *mountain*
monstro, are, &c. tr. *show, command*
monstrum, i, n. *portent, monster*
mŏra, ae, f. *delay, straggler*
mŏrĭbundus, a, um, *dying*
mŏrior, mori, mortuus, intr. *die*
mŏror, ari, &c. intr. *delay, pause*
mors, tis, f. *death*
mortālis, e, *mortal*
mos, mōris, m. *manner, custom*, pl. *character;* more, *after manner of*, with gen.
mōtus, ūs, m. *movement*
mŏveo, movēre, mōvi, mōtum, tr. *move, influence*
mox, *soon*
mūgio, ire, ii, itum, intr. *bellow, roar*
multĭplex, plĭcis, adj. *manyfold, varied*
multus, a, um, *much*
mūnus, ĕris, n. *gift*
mūrex, ĭcis, m. *purple-dye*
murmur, ŭris, n. *murmur, noise*
mūrus, i, m. *wall*
mūtabilis, e, *changeable*
mūto, are, &c. tr. *change*

nam, *for*
narro, are, &c. tr. *relate*
nascor, nasci, nātus, intr. dep. *be born*
năto, are, &c. intr. *float*
natus, i, m. *child*
nauta, ae, m. *sailor*
nāvāle, is, n. *dockyard*, pl. in same sense
nāvĭgo, are, &c. intr. *sail*
nāvis, is, f. *ship*
nĕ, enclitic interrog. particle
nē, *lest, that...not*
nec=neque
necdum, *and not yet*
nĕcesse, adj. only used in neut. *necessary*
necto, nectĕre, nexui, nexum, tr. *weave, fetter*
nĕfandus, a, um, *shocking, abominable*
nĕfas, indecl. *that which is forbidden by divine law, sin*
nĕgo, are, &c. tr. *deny, refuse*
nēmo, ĭnis, c. *no one*
nĕmus, ŏris, n. *wood*
nĕpos, ōtis, m. *grandson, descendant*
nĕque, *both not...and not, neither...nor*
nēquīquam, *in vain*

nescio, ire, ivi and ii, itum, tr. *not know*
nescius, a, um, *ignorant*
nĭger, gra, grum, *black*
nĭgrans, tis, part. of nigro, *black*
nigresco, grescĕre, grui, intr. *grow black*
nihil, nil, *nothing*
nimbus, i, m. *storm cloud*
nimium, *too*
nītor, niti, nixus and nisus, intr. dep. *strive, work*
nĭveus, a, um, *snowy*
nix, nĭvis, f. *snow*
nocturnus, a, um, *by night*
nōdo, are, &c. tr. *knot*
Nŏmas, ădis, m. *nomad, Numidian*
nōn, *not*, nondum, *not yet*
nosco, noscĕre, nōvi, nōtum, tr. *learn*, perf. *know*
noster, tra, trum, *our*
nŏvo, are, &c. *make new*
nŏvus, a, um, *new*
nox, ctis, f. *night*
nūbilus, a, um, *cloudy*, n. pl. as subst. *clouds*
nullus, a, um, *none, no*
nūmen, ĭnis, n. *divinity, divine presence*
Numidae, arum, m. *Numidians*
numquam, *never*
nunc, *now*
nuntius, i, m. nuntia, ae, f. *messenger*
nusquam, *nowhere*
nūto, are, &c. intr. *nod*
nūtrix, īcis, f. *nurse*
nympha, ae, f. *nymph*

ōbĭcio, icĕre, ieci, iectum, tr. *throw in the way, expose*
ŏbĭtus, ūs, m. *death*
oblīviscor, livisci, lītus, intr. dep. *be forgetful*
obmūtesco, tescĕre, tui, intr. *be struck dumb*
obnītor, niti, nixus, intr. dep. *use strong effort*
ŏbŏrior, oriri, ortus, intr. dep. *rise in spite of effort to prevent*, obortus, *rebellious*
obscēnus, a, um, *revolting, foul*
obscūrus, a, um, *dim*
obsto, stare, stiti, intr. *stand in the way*
obstrŭo, struĕre, struxi, structum, tr. *block, stop*
occŭpo, are, &c. tr. *seize, fill*
Ōcĕănus, i, m. *ocean*
ōcius, comp. adv. *swiftly*
ŏcŭlus, i, m. *eye*
ōdi, odisse, defect. tr. *hate*
ŏdium, i, n. *hatred*
ŏdōrus, a, um, *scented, keen scented*
offĕro, offerre, obtŭli, oblātum, tr. *present*
ōlim, *hereafter*
olle, old form of ille
Olympus, i, m. mountain on which the gods dwelt, *the heavens*
ōmen, ĭnis, n. *omen*
omnīno, *altogether*
omnīpŏtens, tis, adj. *all-powerful*
omnis, e, *all, every*
ŏnĕro, are, &c. tr. *load*
ŏpăcus, a, um, *dark*
ŏpĕrio, perire, perui, pertum, tr. *cover*
ops, ŏpis, f. *aid*, pl. *resources, power*
opto, are, &c. tr. *wish, pray*

ŏpus, ĕris, n. *work*
ōra, ae, f. *edge, shore*
orbis, is, m. *circle*, = orbis terrarum, *world*
Orcus, i, m. *Orcus*, the underworld
Orestes, is, m. *Orestes*, son of Agamemnon
orgia, orum, n. pl. *mysterious religious rites*
Orīon, ōnis, *Orion*, constellation, rising and setting of which was accompanied by stormy weather
ornus, i, f. *ash-tree*
ōro, are, &c. tr. *pray, crave*
ortus, ūs, m. *rising*
os, ōris, n. *face, mien*
os, ossis, n. *bone*
ostendo, tendĕre, tendi, tentum, tr. *show*
ostento, are, &c. tr. *show frequently, display*
ostrum, i, n. *purple*
ōtium, i, n. *leisure, idle hours*
ŏvīle, is, n. *sheepfold*
ŏvo, are, &c. intr. *rejoice, triumph*

păciscor, cisci, ctus, intr. *make compact*, perf. partic. in passive sense
palleo, ēre, ui, intr. *be pale*, only in pres. partic.
pallĭdus, a, um, *pale*
pallor, ōris, m. *pallor*
păpāver, ĕris, n. *poppy*
par, păris, adj. *equal*, adv. pariter
părens, tis, c. *parent*
pāreo, ēre, ui, itum, intr. *be obedient*
Părĭs, idis, m. *Paris*, son of Priam, seducer of Helen
păro, are, &c. *get ready, plan*
pars, tis, f. *part*
parvŭlus, a, um, *tiny*
parvus, a, um, *small*
passim, *in all directions*
pastor, ōris, m. *shepherd*
păteo, ēre, ui, intr. *lie open*
păter, tris, m. *father*
pătĕra, ae, f. *flat cup, saucer*, used in sacrifice
pătior, pati, passus, tr. *endure*
pătria, ae, f. *fatherland*
pătrius, a, um, *belonging to a father, to a native land*
paucus, a, um, *small*, pl. *few*
paulum, *little, for a short while*
pax, pācis, f. *peace*
pectus, ŏris, n. *heart, breast*
pĕcus, ŏris, n. *cattle* (collect.)
pĕcus, ŭdis, f. *head of cattle*
pĕlăgus, i, n. *ocean*
Pĕnātes, um, m. pl. *household gods*
pendeo, ēre, pĕpendi, intr. *hang*
pĕnĕtrālis, e, *innermost*
penna, ae, f. *wing*
per, *through, from...to*
pĕrăgo, agĕre, ēgi, actum, tr. *go through with, accomplish*
pĕrăgro, are, &c. tr. *roam*
percŭtio, cutĕre, cussi, cussum, tr. *strike deeply, smite*
perdo, dĕre, dĭdi, ditum, tr. *lose*; perditus, *lost, forlorn*
pĕreo, ire, ivi and ii, ĭtum, intr. *perish*
pĕrerro, are, &c. tr. *wander over, peruse, survey*
perfĕro, ferre, tŭli, lātum, tr. *bear to the end*
perficio, ficĕre, fēci, fectum, tr. *accomplish, finish*

perfĭdus, a, um, *treacherous*

Pergăma, orum, n. pl. *Citadel* of Troy

pergo, pergĕre, perrexi, perrectum, intr. *move forwards, go on*

pĕrhĭbeo, hibēre, hibui, hibitum, tr. *relate*

pĕrīcŭlum, i, n. *peril*

periūrium, i, n. *falsehood*

permitto, mittĕre, mīsi, missum, tr. *commit*

pernix, īcis, adj. *swift*

perpĕtuus, a, um, *lasting, all through*

persentio, sentire, sensi, sensum, tr. *perceive clearly*

pertaedet, taesum est, impers., acc. of pers. gen. of thing, *be sick, weary of*

pes, pĕdis, m. *foot*

pestis, is, f. *plague, bane, danger*

pĕto, petĕre, petivi and petii, petītum, tr. *seek*

phărĕtra, ae, f. *quiver*

Phoebēus, a, um, *of Phoebus*, Apollo

Phoenissa, ae, fem. adj. *Phenician, Carthaginian*

Phrȳgius, a, um, *Trojan, Asiatic, Phrygian*

Phryx, ȳgis, m. *a Phrygian, Trojan*

plăcŭlum, i, n. *expiatory rite* or *sacrifice*

pĭget, ēre, uit, impers. with acc. and infin., me piget, *I am disinclined, I find no pleasure*

pingo, pingĕre, pinxi, pictum, tr. *paint, embroider*

pinguis, e, *fat, rich, fertile*

pīnĭfer, era, erum, *pine-bearing*

pinna, ae, f. *wing, pinion*

piscōsus, a, um, *full of fish, fish-haunted*

pius, a, um, *good-hearted*

plăceo, ēre, ui, itum, intr. *be pleasing*, pf. part. in neut. sense, *pleasing*

plăcĭdus, a, um, *calm, kindly*

plăga, ae, f. *net*

plangor, ōris, m. *beating of the breast, loud mourning*

planta, ae, f. *sole of the foot, foot*

plūma, ae, f. *feather*

plūrimus, a, um, superl. of multus

poena, ae, f. *penalty*

Poenus, a, um, *Carthaginian*

pŏlus, i, m. *sky*

pōno, ponĕre, posui, positum, tr. *place, build, lay*

pŏpŭlo, are, &c. tr. *plunder, carry off, loot*

pŏpŭlus, i, m. *nation, people*

porta, ae, f. *gate*

porto, are, &c. tr. *carry*

portus, ūs, m. *harbour*

posco, poscĕre, pŏposci, tr. *ask, demand*, with double accus.

possum, posse, pŏtŭi, intr. *be able*

post, prep. and adv. *after, behind*, postquam, conj. *after, when*

postĕrus, a, um, *following, next*

pŏtestas, ātis, f. *power*

pŏtior, us, *preferable*, neut. used as adv. *rather*

pŏtior, iri, itus, intr. dep. *be master, gain possession*, with abl.

praeceps, cipitis, adj. *headlong*
praecipito, are, &c. intr. *go headlong, run*
praeclārus, a, um, *renowned*
praeda, ae, f. *booty*
praedictum, i, n. *prophecy*
praemium, i, n. *reward*
praeripio, ripĕre, ripui, reptum, tr. *seize first*, or *before another*
praesentio, sentire, sensi, sensum, tr. *perceive first, scent*
praetendo, tendĕre, tendi, tentum, tr. *hold out before, use as screen*
praetĕrĕā, *besides*
praetereo, ire, ii, ĭtum, tr. *pass*
praetexo, texĕre, texui, textum, tr. *veil*
prāvus, a, um, *distorted, wrong, false*
prĕcor, ari, &c. tr. dep. *pray*
prĕmo, premĕre, pressi, pressum, tr. *press, hide, confine*
prĕtium, i, n. *price*
Priămus, i, m. *Priam*, king of Troy at the time of the Trojan war
prex, prĕcis, f. *prayer*
prīmus, a, um, *first*
princĭpium, i, n. *beginning*
prior, us, *former*; prius, adv. *sooner, before*
prō, *in accordance with*
prō! interj. *Oh! ah!*
prŏbo, are, &c. tr. *approve*
prōcēdo, cedĕre, cessi, cessum, intr. *advance*
prŏcul, *afar off*
prŏcus, i, m. *suitor*
prōdo, dĕre, dĭdi, dĭtum, tr. *send forth, begin, abandon, betray*
prŏficiscor, ficisci, fectus, intr. dep. *set forth, issue*
prōfor, ari, &c. tr. dep. *speak*
prŏfundus, a, um, *deep*
prōgigno, gignĕre, gĕnui, genitum, tr. *give birth to*
prōgrĕdior, grĕdi, gressus, intr. *walk forth*
prōles, is, f. *stock, offspring*
prōmereor, ēri, ĭtus, intr. dep. *render service*
prōmitto, mittĕre, mīsi, missum, tr. *promise, engage*
prōnŭbus, a, um, *forwarding marriage*, epithet of Juno, patron-power of wedlock, but see n. 166
prŏpĕro, are, &c. intr. *hasten*
prŏprius, a, um, *one's own*
propter, *on account of*
prōpugnācŭlum, i, n. *rampart*
Prōserpĭna, ae, f. *Proserpine*, wife of Pluto
prospĭcio, spicĕre, spexi, spectum, tr. *look out and see*
proxĭmus, a, um, *nearest*
pūbens, tis, adj. *full of sap, juicy*
pŭdor, ōris, m. *shame, modesty*
pŭer, eri, m. *boy*
pugna, ae, f. *battle*
pugno, are, &c. intr. *fight*
pugnus, i, m. *fist*
pulchĕr, chra, chrum, *beautiful*
pulso, are, &c. tr. *beat*
pulvĕrŭlentus, a, um, *dusty*
Pūnĭcus, a, um, *Carthaginian*
puppis, is, f. *stern, ship*
purpureus, a, um, *purple*
pўra, ae, f. *funeral-pile*

quaero, quaerĕre, quaesīvi, quaesītum, tr. *seek*

quālis, e, *such, as, like*
quam, *how, than;* ante... quam, *sooner than, before*
quando, *since*
quantus, a, um, *as great as, how great*, neut. used as adv.
quasso, are, &c. tr. *shake, batter*
que, *and, both*, enclitic conj.
quercus, ūs, f. *oak*
quĕrella, ae, f. *complaint*
quĕror, queri, questus, tr. *complain*
questus, ūs, m. *complaint*
qui, quae, quod, relat. pron. *who*, interrog. adj. *what?*
quicunque, quaecunque, quodcunque, *whoever, whatever*
quies, ētis, f. *rest*
quiesco, escĕre, ēvi, ētum, intr. *rest*
quiētus, a, um, *at rest*
quin, *why not? nay more*
quippe, *doubtless* (ironical)
quis, quid, interrog. pron. *who?* indef. *anyone*
quisquam, quicquam, *anyone (thing) at all*, in neg. and interrog. sentences
quisquis, quicquid, *whoever, whatever*
quo, *whither, to what end, in order that*
quondam, *formerly*
quŏniam, *since*
quŏque, *also*
quot, indecl. *as many as*
quŏties (ens), *as often as*

răbies, ei, f. *rage*
rădius, i, m. *ray*
rādix, īcis, f. *root*
rāmus, i, m. *branch*
răpidus, a, um, *swift*
răpio, rapĕre, rapui, raptum, *tr. seize, ravish*
raptum, i, n. *plunder*
rārus, a, um, *at intervals, wide-meshed*
rătio, ōnis, f. *way of thinking, method*
rătis, is, f. *bark, ship*
rĕcēdo, cedĕre, cessi, cessum, intr. *depart*
rĕcidīvus, a, um, *revived, renewed*
rĕcingo, cingĕre, cinxi, cinctum, *tr. ungirdle*
rĕcipio, cipĕre, cēpi, ceptum, *tr. receive, recover*
rĕclūdo, cludĕre, clūsi, clūsum, *tr. open, bare*
rĕcurso, are, &c. intr. *come running back*
reddo, dĕre, dĭdi, dĭtum, *tr. restore*
rĕdūco, ducĕre, duxi, ductum, tr. *bring back, restore*
refello, fellĕre, felli, tr. *contradict, disprove*
rĕfĕro, referre, rettŭli, relātum, *carry back, reproduce, reply, win*
rēgīna, ae, f. *queen*
rĕgio, ōnis, f. *region*
rēgius, a, um, *royal*
regnātor, ōris, m. *ruler*
regnum, i, n. *kingdom*, pl. in same sense
rĕgo, regĕre, rexi, rectum, tr. *direct, rule*
rĕlinquo, linquĕre, līqui, lictum, tr. *leave, abandon*
rĕliquiae, arum, f. pl. *relics*
rēmex, igis, m. *rower*
rĕmitto, mittĕre, mīsi, missum, tr. *send back, return*
rēmus, i, m. *oar*

rĕor, rēri, rătus, tr. dep. *think*
rĕpello, repellĕre, reppuli, repulsum, *tr. repel, reject*
rĕpĕrio, reperire, repperi, repertum, *tr. discover*
rĕplĕo, ēre, ēvi, ētum, tr. *fill full*
rĕpōno, ponĕre, posui, positum, tr. *replace, deposit*
rĕquies, requiem, f. *rest*
rēs, rĕi, f. *any object of thought, thing*
rĕservo, are, &c. tr. *keep back, reserve*
rĕsigno, are, &c. tr. see note 244
rĕsisto, sistĕre, stĭti, intr. *stand still, stop, resist*
rĕsolvo, solvĕre, solvi, solūtum, tr. *loosen, relax*
rĕsŏno, are, intr. *resound*
respĭcio, spicĕre, spexi, spectum, *tr. look back for, regard*
resto, stare, stĭti, intr. *remain*
rĕsurgo, surgĕre, surrexi, surrectum, intr. *rise again*
rēte, is, n. *net*
rĕtĕgo, tegĕre, texi, tectum, *tr. uncover*
rĕtĭnācŭlum, i, n. *cable, hawser*
rĕtro, *backwards*
rĕvello, vellĕre, velli, volsum, tr. *tear off, away*
rĕvincio, vincire, vinxi, vinctum, *tr. bind, wreathe*
rĕvīso, visĕre, tr. *revisit*
rĕvŏco, are, &c. tr. *recall*
rĕvolvo, volvĕre, volvi, volutum, tr. *roll back*
rex, rēgis, m. *king*
rīdeo, dēre, si, sum, intr. *laugh*
rĭgeo, ēre, intr. *be stiff*
rītē, *duly*
rōbur, ŏris, n. *oak, timber*
rŏgus, i, m. *funeral-pile*
Rōmānus, a, um, *Roman*
roscĭdus, a, um, *dewy*
rūmor, ōris, m. *rumour*
rumpo, rumpĕre, rūpi, ruptum, *tr. break, burst, let burst*
rŭo, ruĕre, intr. *rush*
rursus, *again*
rus, rūris, n. *field*

săcer, cra, crum, *sacred, consecrated*
săcerdos, ōtis, c. *priest, priestess*
sacro, āre, &c. tr. *consecrate*
sacrum, i, n. *sacrifice*
saepe, *often*
saevio, ire, ii, itum, intr. *be cruel, vent wrath*
saevus, a, um, *cruel*
săgitta, ae, f. *arrow*
saltem, *at least*
saltus, ūs, m. *glade*
sanctus, a, um, *hallowed, holy*
sanguĭneus, a, um, *bloodshot*
sanguis, ĭnis, m. *blood*
sānus, a, um, *sound, healthy,* in body or mind
Sāturnius, a, um, *belonging to, child of Saturn*
saucius, a, um, *wounded*
saxum, i, n. *stone*
scaena, ae, f. *scene, stage*
sceptrum, i, n. *sceptre,* generally in pl.
scĭlĭcet, *doubtless* (ironical)
scŏpŭlus, i, m. *rock*
se (sese), sui, sibi, reflexive pron. 3rd pers. sing. and pl.
sĕco, secare, secui, sectum, tr. *cut*

sēcrētus, a, um, *secret, in secret*
sĕcundus, a, um, *following, favorable*
sĕcus, *otherwise*
sed, *but*
sĕdeo, sedēre, sēdi, sessum, intr. *sit*
sēdes, is, f. *seat, abode*
sēdūco, ducĕre, duxi, ductum, tr. *withdraw, divide*
segnis, e, *slow, ungraceful*
sēmiănimis, e, *half-dead*
sēmĭta, ae, f. *path*
sēmĭvir, vĭri, m. *half-man, womanish*
semper, *always*
sĕnex, senis, *old*, subst. *old man*
sensus, ūs, m. *feeling*
sententia, ae, *opinion, resolve*
sentio, tire, si, sum, tr. *feel, think, perceive*
sĕpĕlio, pelire, pelivi, pultum, tr. *bury*
sĕpulchrum, i, n. *tomb*
sĕquor, sequi, secūtus, tr. dep. *follow*
sĕrēno, are, &c. tr. *brighten*
sermo, ōnis, m. *talking*
sĕro, rĕre, sēvi, sătum, tr. *sow*
serpens, tis, m. *serpent*
sertum, i, n. *garland*
servio, ire, ivi and ii, itum, intr. *be slave, subject*
servo, are, &c. tr. *guard, keep*
seu=sive
si, *if*
sīc, *thus*
sicco, are, &c. tr. *dry, stanch*
Sīdŏnius, a, um, *Sidonian, Phenician*
sīdus, ĕris, n. *star*
signum, i, n. *signal*
sĭleo, ēre, ui, intr. *be silent*
silva, ae, f. *forest*
sĭmĭlis, e, *like*
sĭmŭl, *at the same time;* simul atque (ac), *as soon as*
sĭmŭlo, are, &c. tr. *pretend*
sĭnĕ, *without*
sĭno, sinĕre, sīvi, tr. *permit*
sĭnus, ūs, m. *fold of garment, bosom*
sisto, sistĕre, tr. *make to stand, stay, fetch*
sĭtis, is, f. *thirst*
sīve, *whether...or, either if... or if*
sŏcio, are, &c. tr. *unite*
sŏcius, i (gen. pl. -um), m. *comrade*
sol, sōlis, m. *sun*
sollĭcĭto, are, &c. tr. *disquiet*
sōlor, ari, &c. tr. dep. *console*
sŏlum, i, n. *ground, floor*
sōlus, a, um, *alone*
solvo, solvĕre, solvi, sŏlūtum, tr. *loosen, release, set free, break down*
somnus, i, m. *sleep*
sŏnĭpes, pēdis, *sounding with the feet;* subst. *palfrey*
sŏpor, ōris, m. *slumber*
sŏpōrĭfer, era, erum, *sleep-giving*
sŏror, ōris, f. *sister*
sors, tis, f. *lot*, pl. *oracle*
spargo, spargĕre, sparsi, sparsum, tr. *sprinkle*
spătĭor, ari, &c. intr. dep. *pace*
spătĭum, i, n. *course, space, time*
spĕcies, ei, f. *appearance, form*
spĕcula, ae, f. *watch-tower*
spēlunca, ae, f. *cave*
sperno, spernĕre, sprēvi, sprētum, tr. *reject, scorn*

spēro, are, &c. tr. *expect*, *hope*
spes, ei, f. *hope*
spīritus, ūs, m. *breath*, *life*
spīro, are, &c. intr. *breathe*
spŏlium, i, n. *spoil*
sponte, *willingly*
spūmo, are, &c. intr. *foam*
stăbilis, e, *lasting*
stătŭo, uĕre, ui, ūtum, tr. *make to stand*, *set*, *found*
stella, ae, f. *star*
stellātus, a, um, *starred*
stĭmŭlo, are, &c. tr. *spur*
stīpes, ĭtis, m. *stem*, *trunk*
stīpo, are, &c. tr. *throng*
stirps, pis, f. *stock*, *race*, *lineage*
sto, stāre, stĕti, stătum, intr. *stand*
strātum, i, n. *couch*, pl. in same sense
strīdo (strideo), ĕre, intr. *hiss*
strīdor, ōris, m. *noise*, *roar*, *groaning*
stringo, stringĕre, strinxi, strictum, tr. *touch lightly*, *draw one thing lightly against another*, *unsheath*
strŭo, struĕre, struxi, structum, tr. *form*, *plan*
stŭdium, i, n. *eager desire*, *zest*
Stȳgius, a, um, *of the Styx*
suādeo, dēre, si, sum, tr. *advise*
sub, *under*
sŭbeo, ire, ii, ĭtum, tr. *undergo*, *lift* (a burden)
sŭbĭtus, a, um, *sudden*
sublīmis, e, *uplifted*, *towering*
submitto, mittĕre, mīsi, missum, tr. *lower*, *submit*
subnecto, nectĕre, nexui, nexum, tr. *tie beneath*
subnītor, niti, nixus, intr. *rest on*
sŭbŏles, is, f. *offspring*
subrīdeo, dēre, si, sum, intr. *smile*
subrīgo, gĕre, tr. *erect*
subter, adv. *underneath*
succēdo, cedĕre, cessi, cessum, intr. *enter*
succumbo, cumbĕre, cubui, cŭbitum, intr. *fall prostrate*, *yield*
sum, esse, fui, *be*
summa, ae, f. *sum total*
summus, a, um, *topmost*
sūmo, sumĕre, sumpsi, sumptum, tr. *take*
sŭper, adv. *above*, prep. *on behalf of*
sŭperbus, a, um, *proud*
sŭpĕrinpōno, ponĕre, posui, positum, tr. *lay above*
sŭpĕrus, a, um, *upper*, *above*; superi, *gods*
sŭpīnus, a, um, *on the back*, *upturned*
supplex, ĭcis, adj. *suppliant*
supplĭcium, i, n. *punishment*
supra, *above*
surgo, surgĕre, surrexi, surrectum, intr. *rise*
suscĭpiŏ, cipĕre, cēpi, ceptum, tr. *undertake*, *take up*
suspensus, a, um (pass. partic. suspendo), *fluttering*, *agitated*
suspĭcio, spicĕre, spexi, spectum, tr. *look at from underneath*, *suspect*, *mislike*
sŭus, a, um, *his*, *her*, *their own*
Sȳchaeus, i, m. first husband of Dido
Syrtis, is, f. *Syrtis*, quicksand on N. Coast of Africa

tăceo, ēre, ui, itum, intr. *be silent*
tăcitus, a, um, *silent*
taeda, ae, f. *torch*, *marriage-torch*
taedet, ēre, impers. acc. and gen. *be tired of*
tālāria, ium, n. pl. *ancle-wings*
tālis, e, *such*
tam, *so*, *as*
tămĕn, *nevertheless*, *in spite of all*
tandem, *at length*, (rhetorical) *I ask!*
tango, tangĕre, tĕtīgi, tactum, tr. *touch*
tantus, a, um, *so great; tantum*, *only*
Tartăra, orum, n. pl. *Infernal regions*
tectum, i, n. *shelter*, *house*
tĕgo, tegĕre, texi, tectum, *tr. cover*
tēla, ae, f. *web*
tellus, ūris, f. *earth*
tēlum, i, n. *missile weapon*
templum, i, n. *temple*
tempto, are, &c. tr. *make trial of*, *essay*
tempus, ŏris, n. *time*, *temple* (of the head)
tĕnax, ācis, adj. *tenacious*
tendo, tendĕre, tĕtendi, tentum and tensum, intr. *stretch*, *extend*
tĕnĕo, tenĕre, tenui, tentum, tr. *hold*
tĕnuis, e, *thin*, *fine*
ter, *thrice*
tergĕminus, a, um, *triple*
terminus, i, m. *boundary*
tĕro, terĕre, trīvi, trītum, tr. *wear*, *spend*
terra, ae, f. *land*
terreo, ēre, ui, itum, tr. *alarm*
terrĭbilis, e, *terrifying*
terrifico, are, &c. tr. *terrify*
terrĭto, are, &c. tr. *scare*
testor, ari, &c. tr. dep. *call to witness*
Teucri, orum *and* ûm, *Trojans*
thălămus, i, m. *marriage-bed*, *chamber*, *wedlock*
Thyias (dissyllable), ădis, f. *Thyiad*, *Bacchante*
tigris, is and ĭdis, acc. tigrim, f. *tigress*
tĭmeo, ēre, ui, tr. *fear*
tĭmor, ōris, m. *fear*, *cowardice*
Tītan, ānis, m. *Titan*, esp. *the* Titan, the sun, son of Hyperion and Thea
Tīthōnus, i, m. husband of Aurora
tŏnĭtru, ūs, n. *thunder*
tŏno, are, ui, itum, intr. *thunder*
torqueo, quēre, si, tum, tr. *turn*, *hurl*, *twist*
tŏrus, i, m. *couch*
tot, indecl. *so many*
tŏtĭdem, indecl. *just so many*
tŏtiens, *so many times*
tōtus, a, um, *whole*
trabs, trăbis, f. *trunk* (of a tree), *ship*
tractābĭlis, e, *capable of being worked by the hand*, *manageable*, *pliant;* by metaph. (of the sky) non *tr. impracticable*, *forbidding*, (of a man) *unyielding*
trādo, dĕre, dĭdi, dĭtum, tr. *surrender*, *submit*
trăho, trahĕre, traxi, tractum, tr. *drag*, *draw*

trāno, are, &c. tr. *float, swim across*
transmitto, mittĕre, mīsi, missum, tr. *traverse*
transtrum, i, n. *rowing-bench*
trĕmo, ĕre, ui, intr. *tremble, quiver*
trĕpĭdo, are, &c. intr. *be alarmed, hurry*
trĕpĭdus, a, um, *trembling, excited*
tres, tria, *three*
triĕtērĭcus, a, um, *recurring every three years*
tristis, e, *sad, gloomy*
trĭumphus, i, m. *triumphal procession, triumph*
trĭvĭum, i, n. *junction of three roads*
Troia, ae, f. *Troy*
Troiānus, a, um, *Trojan*
Trōs, ōĭs, m. *a Trojan*
trūdo, dĕre, si, sum, tr. *push*
tū, tŭi, &c. second pers. pron.
tŭba, ae, f. *trumpet*
tŭĕor, ēri, ĭtus, tr. *look at, eye*
tum, *then*
tundo, tundĕre, tŭtŭdi, tunsum, tr. *beat heavily*
turbĭdus, a, um, *stormy, wild, angry*
turbo, are, &c. tr. *disturb, set in uproar*
tūrĭcrĕmus, a, um, *incense-burning*
turpis, e, *base, disgraceful*
turris, is, f. *tower*
tūtus, a, um, *safe*
tŭus, a, um, *thy*
tўrannus, i, m. *monarch*
Tўrius, a, um, *Tyrian*
Tўrus, i, f. *Tyre*

ūber, ĕris, n. *teat*
ŭbĭ, *when, where*
ulciscor, cisci, tus, tr. dep. *avenge*
ultimus, a, um, *last*
ultor, ōris, m. *avenger*
ultrix, īcis, f. adj. *avenging*
ultro, *beyond* (what would naturally be expected), *unasked, unchallenged, first, even, actually*, cf. Ecl. VIII. 52, Aen. II. 145, X. 282, IX. 7, 127
ŭlŭlātus, ūs, m. *loud crying* (esp. of women)
ŭlŭlo, are, &c. intr. *wail*
umbra, ae, f. *shade*
ūmeo, ēre, intr. *be wet*
ŭmĕrus, i, m. *shoulder*
ūmĭdus, a, um, *wet*
umquam, *ever, at any time*
ūnā, *together*
unanimus, a, um, *one-souled, sympathising*
unda, ae, f. *wave, water*
undĭque, *from all sides*
undōsus, a, um, *full of waves*
unguis, is, m. *nail*
unguo, unguĕre, unxi, unctum, tr. *smear, caulk*
ūnus, a, um, *one*
urbs, bis, f. *city*
ūro, ĕre, ussi, ustum, tr. *burn*
ūsus, ūs, m. *use, service*
ut, *as, when*
ŭterque, traque, trumque, *each* (of two)
uxōrius, a, um, *uxorious, thrall of a woman*

vacca, ae, f. *cow*
văcŭus, a, um, *empty*
vādo, dĕre, intr. *go*
vāgīna, ae, f. *sheath*
văleo, ēre, ui, intr. *be strong*

vălĭdus, a, um, *strong*
vallis, is, f. *valley*
vānus, a, um, *ungrounded*
vărĭus, a, um, *varying, changeable*
vātes, is, c. *prophet*
vel, *either, or, even*
vellus, ĕris, n. *fleece*
vēlox, ōcis, adj. *swift*
vēlum, i, n. *sail*
vĕlŭt, *even as*
vēna, ae, f. *vein*
vēnābŭlum, i, n. *hunting-spear*
vĕnēnum, i, n. *poison*
vĕnĭa, ae, f. *indulgence, pardon*
vĕnio, venire, vēni, ventum, intr. *come*
vēnor, ari, &c. intr. dep. *hunt*
ventus, i, m. *wind*
Vĕnus, ĕris, f. *Venus*, goddess of love
verbum, i, n. *word*
vĕrĕor, ēri, ĭtus, tr. dep. *fear*
vĕrō, *truly, in truth* (ironical)
verro, verrĕre, verri, versum, tr. *sweep*
verso, are, &c. tr. *turn and turn*
vertex, ĭcis, m. *crest, head*
verto, tĕre, ti, sum, tr. *turn*
vērum, *but*
vestīgĭum, i, n. *footstep*
vestis, is, f. *garment*
vĕtus, ĕris, adj. *old*
vexo, are, &c. tr. *harass*
vĭa, ae, f. *road, path*
vĭcissim, *by turns*
vĭdĕo, vidēre, vīdi, vīsum, tr. *see*; videor *seem*
vĭgil, ĭlis, adj. *wakeful, watchful, undying*
vĭgĭlo, are, &c. intr. *wake, watch*
vinco, vincĕre, vīci, victum, tr. *conquer*
vincŭlum (-clum), i, n. *chain*
vindĭco, are, &c. tr. *claim as free, rescue*
vīnum, i, n. *wine*
vĭŏlo, are, &c. tr. *outrage*
vĭr, vĭri (g. pl. virûm), m. *man*
virga, ae, f. *rod, wand*
virgo, ĭnis, f. *maiden*
virtus, ūtis, f. *worth, valour*
vis, vim, vi, f. *force*, vīres, ium, *strength*
vīsus, ūs, m. *sight*
vīta, ae, f. *life*
vitta, ae, f. *fillet*
vīvo, vivĕre, vixi, victum, intr. *live*
vŏco, āre, &c. tr. *call, call on*
vŏlātilis, e, *flying*
volnus, ĕris, n. *wound*
vŏlo, are, &c. intr. *fly*
vŏlo, velle, volui, tr. *wish*
voltus, ūs, m. *face, look*
vŏlŭcris, is, f. *bird*
vŏluntas, ātis, f. *will*
vŏlūto, are, &c. tr. *revolve*
volvo, volvĕre, volvi, volūtum, tr. *roll, revolve*
vōtum, i, n. *vow, prayer*
vox, vōcis, f. *voice, words*

Xanthus, i, m. river in Lycia

zĕphўrus, i, m. *west-wind, breeze*

CAMBRIDGE: PRINTED BY C. J. CLAY, M.A. & SONS, AT THE UNIVERSITY PRESS.

Lightning Source UK Ltd.
Milton Keynes UK
UKHW011426050119
334992UK00007B/86/P